MEASURING
TOMORROW

MEASURING TOMORROW

Accounting for Well-Being, Resilience, and Sustainability in the Twenty-First Century

ÉLOI LAURENT

PRINCETON UNIVERSITY PRESS

Princeton and Oxford

Copyright © 2018 by Princeton University Press

Published by Princeton University Press,
41 William Street, Princeton, New Jersey 08540

In the United Kingdom: Princeton University Press,
6 Oxford Street, Woodstock, Oxfordshire OX20 1TR

press.princeton.edu

Jacket design by C. Alvarez-Gaffin
Jacket images courtesy of Shutterstock

ISBN 978-0-691-17069-5
Library of Congress Control Number: 2017956545

British Library Cataloging-in-Publication Data is available

This book has been composed in Charis SIL

Printed on acid-free paper. ∞

Printed in the United States of America

1 3 5 7 9 10 8 6 4 2

To Sylvie, for Sylvie, by Sylvie,

my sustainable well-being

To Lila and Jonas, my tomorrows

All things are number.

—*Pythagoras*

Not everything that can be counted counts,
and not everything that counts can be counted.

—*William Bruce Cameron*

Contents

Part III
Managing the Well-Being and Sustainability Transition

List of Illustrations

FIGURES

TABLES

Acknowledgments

I want, first and foremost, to warmly thank all of my students who, for the last twenty years, have educated me in many ways. My classes and teaching assistants at Stanford, Harvard, and Sciences Po over the last five years deserve special thanks, for they have directly shaped the content of this book. Trailblazing scholars, chief among them Dominique Méda, Jean Gadrey, and Florence Jany-Catrice, convinced me, a conventional macroeconomist by training, that GDP and growth were problems and not solutions. Lin Ostrom and Jim Boyce have profoundly influenced my social-ecological thinking, helping me understand how well-being is related to sustainability. Jacques Le Cacheux has been a terrific coauthor and co-teacher over the years. Amartya Sen, Bob Solow, Ken Arrow, and Joe Stiglitz have been lifelong inspiring figures. Institutions and colleagues at Stanford University and Harvard University have played a key role in bringing this book to life. At Stanford, within the SEWSS program in Y2E2 and at the Stanford University program in Paris, Jim Leckie, Colin Ong, and Estelle Halévi have been wonderful hosts and coeducators. At Harvard's Center for European Studies and in its environmental science and public policy concentration, Michèle Lamont, Peter Hall, and Bill Clark have shared their immense knowledge with simple generosity. My home institutions in Paris, OFCE and Sciences Po, have provided continuing support and uniquely vibrant environments. I thank two anonymous referees who gave me the chance to make this book considerably better. Finally, a very special thank you to Sarah Caro at Princeton University Press, who made the journey of this book one of the most enjoyable of my professional life.

MEASURING
TOMORROW

Introduction

Values, Data, and Indicators

We are living an empirical revolution. Humans have never produced so much data (2.5 quintillion bytes a day), and data have never been so powerful in organizing societies and determining policy. From an economist's point of view, this revolution is a daily business: in the last twenty years, both economic research and economic policy have been deluged with data. A 2013 study showed that up to two-thirds of the articles published in top journals are now empirical compared to fewer than 30 percent ranked as theoretical.[1] The ascent of "datanomics," literally an age when data rule, is thus an undeniable reality, but it is not without peril: the democratic governments of our data-driven societies require the development of data literacy, which is precisely what this book aims to help do.

Let's start with the basic idea that data are not, as their derivation from Latin might suggest, a given, but are, in fact, a social construct, behind which lies a particular vision of the world and a specific methodology. Data, instruments of knowledge, result from hypotheses, models, and techniques, but they are also tainted by norms, values, and even ideology. In the hands of policy makers, they become instruments of power or "indicators." (The etymology here is "index," the finger that points to an object or a direction.)

The starting point of this book is therefore that, contrary to their etymology, data are the product of values, which in turn influence human attitudes and behaviors via policy when they become indicators by the combined action of scholars and policy makers. As Donatella Meadows put it, "Indicators arise from values (we measure what we care about), and they create values (we care about what we measure)."[2] The main purpose of *Measuring Tomorrow* is to show that we currently govern our economies with the wrong indicators because they divert our attention away from the real challenges of the early twenty-first century. The issue is less the size of our ever-expanding empirical universe as the quality of the data that populate it. In other words, rather than being excited to live in the era of "big data," we should be concerned that we are living in the era of "bad data."

Because data are instruments of both knowledge and power,[3] they can be both vectors of change and reform and tools of stability and order. In this regard, economics has been a force of inertia in the last few decades, imposing a certain vision of the social world whereby some indicators (sustained by certain values) dominate others and have a strong influence on collective choices while hardly, if ever, being publicly debated or deconstructed. Indicators such as the growth rate of the gross domestic product or the stock market index profoundly influence government policy and citizens' daily lives, while many crucial dimensions of human activities are neither measured, monitored, nor managed.

In the last three decades or so, a period when economics has been dominated by increasingly standardized models, methodologies, and metrics (a situation that was only briefly contested during and shortly after the "great recession" of 2008–2009), three critical issues in particular have been widely overlooked: well-being, resilience, and sustainability.

The concern for well-being (or welfare) stems from an eternal question: what are the real drivers of human development and success apart from material conditions? Exploring human well-being means articulating a multidimensional vision of human welfare casually referred to as "quality of life." Human well-being can be assessed at different geographic scales, or objectively (via measures of health status or educational attainments), or subjectively (through the assessment of happiness or trust), but it is in all cases a static metric that tells us nothing about its evolution over time.

For a dynamic approach that sheds light not only on the current state of well-being but also on its future, one has to turn to the concepts of resilience and sustainability. The questions asked by citizens and policy makers then become substantially more complex: "Can we project our well-being over time? How?"

Resilience is a first step in this direction, as it tries to determine if well-being can resist and survive shocks. More precisely, it assesses the ability of a community, a locality, a nation, or the whole planet to cope with economic, social, or environmental shocks and their capacity to return afterward to their pre-shock level of well-being without seeing it degraded or destroyed. One typical, pressing resilience issue is how human communities around the world can adapt to climate change.

The measurement—or, more accurately, assessment[4]—of sustainability is even more ambitious, in that it seeks to evaluate well-being in the long run, both after the occurrence of shocks and during normal times. Some economists view human societies as holders and managers of stocks of capital from which they derive benefits and that determine their long-term development: manufactured capital (factories, cities, infrastructures), human capital (population, health, education), social capital (institutions governing social interactions and norms of trust), knowledge capital (scientific discoveries, technology, talents), and natural capital (climate, soil, biodiversity, minerals).

Attempting to assess sustainability is about trying to understand how these stocks can be maintained or even increased over time, such as how services freely provided by ecosystems can continue benefiting future generations. (Consider, for example, pollination, on which 75 percent of the world's crops at least partially depend.) From this perspective, resilience can be understood as the short-run horizon of sustainability: resilience is concerned with shocks and sustainability with stocks. In our "environmental century" (a phrase coined by E. O. Wilson), the key message of sustainability analysis is that human development is nothing more than a temporary illusion if it cannot be maintained over time and reconciled with current and future ecological constraints.

In my view, the whole of economic activity, which is a subset of social cooperation, should be reoriented toward the well-being of citizens and the resilience and sustainability of societies. For that to happen, we need to put these three collective horizons at the center of our empirical world. Or rather, back at the center. Issues of well-being and sustainability have been around for quite a long time in economic analysis and were a central part of its philosophy until the end of the nineteenth century. Contemporary economics has largely forgotten that these concerns were once at the core of its reflections.

Well-being was at the heart of Greek philosophy and the explicit starting point of ethical considerations by Aristotle, the founding father of economic reasoning. For him, economics meant the management of the scarce resources within the household (*oikos, nomos*)—what we now call microeconomics—and its ultimate goal, as described in the first chapter of *The Nicomachean Ethics,* was not income accumulation, but happiness:

> Suppose, then, that there is some end of the thing we pursue in our actions which we wish for because of itself, and because of which we wish for the other things . . . As far as its name goes, most people virtually agree [about what the good is], since both the many and the cultivated call it happiness, and suppose that living well and doing well are the same as being happy . . .[5]

A successful life was, for Aristotle, a happy life, and he conceived economics as a means to this end. In the modern era, when Jeremy Bentham invented utilitarianism, on which so much of the neoclassical economics that emerged at the turn of the twentieth century is still based, he chose to ground his theory on the same belief, writing that "it is the greatest happiness of the greatest number that is the measure of right and wrong."[6] In other words, when economics was born and later modernized, well-being, not income or growth, was its main goal.

What is true of well-being is also true of sustainability. The goal of growing economies within the physical limits of nature, or "planetary boundaries," is, in fact, nothing new. The physiocrats of mid-eighteenth-century France, as represented by Anne-Robert-Jacques Turgot and François Quesnay, thought that power (*cratos*) belonged to those in charge of managing natural resources (*phusis*). Thomas Malthus soon after described with fatalism the precariousness of humans engaged in a great race between the geometrical growth of population and the arithmetical growth of subsistence. This, in turn, influenced David Ricardo, who did not conceive of economic activity outside of the "avarice of Nature," which determined his theory of diminishing returns. Finally, John Stuart Mill envisioned, at the peak of the first industrial revolution, the transition to a "stationary state" (the "irresistible necessity that the stream of human industry should finally spread itself out into an apparently stagnant sea") as a way to reconcile aspirations for social justice and "human improvement."[7]

What happened to economic analysis to make all these key insights largely forgotten for so long? The shift away from well-being and sustainability happened in two crucial steps. First, at the beginning of the twentieth century, economists decided to divorce their study from philosophy—or, more precisely, from ethics—and make it a science of efficiency, modeled on physics. (This posture was embraced by one of the first presidents of the American Economic Association, Charles F. Dunbar.) Then, after the Second World War, it purported to become the science of growth. Both metamorphoses were symbolized by a single indicator: gross domestic product (GDP). Conceived in the 1930s by Harvard development economist Simon Kuznets to take stock of the Great Depression and improved by a team of British economists around John Maynard Keynes in the midst of the war effort, it was crowned king of all economic data at the Bretton Woods conference in July 1944, when Western nations embraced it as their common currency of power and success.

The power of conventional economics has only grown stronger in social science and the social world. But, at its margins, a well-being and sustainability transition has quietly awakened. In recent years, scholars and policy makers have recognized in increasing numbers that standard economic indicators such as GDP not only create false expectations of perpetual societal growth but are also broken compasses for policy. By attempting to measure well-being, they try to pinpoint the real drivers of human success beyond material conditions. By assembling the building blocks of resilience and sustainability, they engage in an even more daunting task: to understand under what conditions human well-being can be maintained over time, under severe ecological constraints. This endeavor matters for two simple and important reasons. Unmeasurability means invisibility, so that, as the saying goes, "what is not measured is not managed." Conversely, measuring is governing: indicators determine policies and actions.

The well-being and sustainability transition received international recognition in September 2015, when the United Nations embraced a "sustainable development goals" agenda in which GDP growth plays only a marginal role. But the well-being and sustainability transition had been put in motion nearly fifty years previously. In a famous speech at the University of Kansas on March 18, 1968, shortly before his assassination, Robert F. Kennedy explained in very clear and accessible language to American citizens the necessity of going beyond gross national product (a variant of GDP) to capture the full meaning of human development:

> Gross National Product counts air pollution and cigarette advertising, and ambulances to clear our highways of carnage. It counts special locks for our doors and the jails for the people who break them. It counts the destruction of the redwood and the loss of our natural wonder in chaotic sprawl. It counts napalm and counts nuclear warheads and armored cars for the police to fight the riots in our cities. It counts [Charles] Whitman's rifle and [Richard] Speck's knife, and the television programs which glorify violence in order to sell toys to our children. Yet the gross national product does not allow for the health of our children, the quality of their education or the joy of their play. It does not include the beauty of our poetry or the strength of our marriages, the intelligence of our public debate or the integrity of our public officials. It measures neither our wit nor our courage, neither our wisdom nor our learning, neither our compassion nor our devotion to our country, it measures everything in short, except that which makes life worthwhile. And it can tell us everything about America except why we are proud that we are Americans.[8]

Academic research devoted to devising new metrics better able to reflect human aspirations and social success paralleled Kennedy's eloquent and powerful criticism. Economists William Nordhaus and James Tobin suggested in a series of papers published between 1972 and 1973 that "growth" (understood narrowly as the increase of GDP) had become "obsolete" and attempted for the first time to offer not just a theoretical alternative, but an empirical one.[9] Thus was born the "beyond GDP" agenda.

This research and policy making agenda has greatly expanded since then, and gained momentum. To sum up contemporary research, one could say that many scholars and policy makers have come to realize that growth cannot solve either of the major crises that mark the beginning of the early twenty-first century: those of inequality (the growing gap between the haves and the have-nots) and ecology (the alarming degradation of climate, ecosystems, and biodiversity that threatens human well-being). The single minded focus on growth has been a diversion from these two pressing challenges. Kuznets himself, the inventor of GDP, intuited this diversion when he warned policy makers in 1934, "Goals for more growth should specify more growth of what and for what."[10] More than eight decades later, we can refine his statement as a question: more growth of what and for whom? This is especially pressing given our troubled political times.

Well-being, resilience, and sustainability indicators that aim to go beyond GDP (that is, not only beyond standard economic measures, but also standard economic models and analyses) are sometimes perceived or caricatured as amusing diversions. They are much more than that: they are key vectors of democracy. Accurate, relevant measures of well-being and sustainability are the foundations of a sound and genuine public debate on what really matters and how life actually is for ordinary people. By contrast, the growing distance between everyday challenges and a political discourse based on misconceptions of social reality is a poison for democracy. The recent US concern over entering a "post-truth era" where there is a casual disregard for objective facts often overlooks that, in a time of increasing but underestimated inequality, people do live in separate social universes and the most deprived deeply distrust official statistics because they don't feel represented by them. Governing societies with metrics that veil this reality instead of highlighting it can be perilous.

Moreover, these indicators, old and new, are genuine markers of civilization: they help us understand what we do in and to the world; they shed light on our means and our ends; they reveal our true quality of life and warn us of its possible grim future. Standard economic indicators such as GDP may indeed be useful for understanding these realities in part, but it is much too narrow a part, whose relevance is ever shrinking in the face of mounting ecological challenges. If reality can be measured, there is more realism in evaluating ecological crises and their impact on human well-being than in locking ourselves into the excesses of an economic development while blind to its impact on a biosphere on which it ultimately depends.

The much-needed transition toward well-being, resilience, and sustainability is actually already under way. Economic research is devoting far more attention to the question of inequality, while sustainability analysis has made valuable progress in recent years. To take just two examples, to which I will come back to in greater detail later, US scholars and (some) policy makers increasingly realize the importance of paying attention to inequality rather than just growth, while China's leaders acknowledge that sustainability is a much better policy target than explosive economic expansion. But progress toward (or back to) well-being and sustainability needs to be accelerated.

Economics, as I understand it, is the discipline that measures what really matters for human beings and designs incentives that provide tools to policy makers to shape human behaviors and attitudes so that human societies have a chance of reaching the goals they set themselves. At its best, economics measures what counts and provides societies with the means to make it count, among the most powerful of which are good indicators. A *New York Times* columnist was quite right to note in 2015, "It is hard to think of any government investment that would have a greater impact than creating robust ways to measure the quality of our lives."[11] From this perspective, each of this book's three parts seeks to ask and answer a key question. (What defines a good indicator? What good indicators are available beyond GDP to account for well-being and sustainability? How can good indicators of well-being, resilience, and sustainability practically change our world?) In doing so, the book aims to make four contributions to the growing field of well-being and sustainability analysis and policy.

First, while we have several insightful historical accounts of GDP's ascent,[12] we also need to take stock of existing alternatives in a forward-looking way. By the same token, we have plenty of pointed critiques of GDP,[13] but need to address the limitations of the alternative indicators. Dozens of the latter are created or updated each year, but their conceptual and empirical foundations are sometimes obscure or weak.

(What exactly do they measure? How well do they measure it?) This book is not only a (necessarily partial) guide to alternative indicators, but a guide to understanding their meaning, accuracy, and usefulness.

Measuring Tomorrow also attempts to grasp indicators' plurality in an as-yet missing consistent framework so we can better understand the continuum among well-being, resilience, and sustainability. Because this framework breaks down well-being and sustainability into a limited number of fundamental dimensions,[14] it does not impose one best indicator on readers, but rather invites them to select and even design those that matter the most for them.

This book also intends to convince readers, within this framework, that advances in human well-being are fully compatible with environmental sustainability and even that the two are, or at least can be, mutually reinforcing. In doing so, it counters the beliefs that there is an unsurmountable trade-off between well-being and sustainability, that sustainability can exist without well-being, and that well-being does not need to be sustainable. Well-being represents the many dimensions of human development (or, in a more poetic view, human flourishing). Resilience represents well-being under shocks. Sustainability represents dynamic well-being. Linking these three dimensions is an operational way to acknowledge the continuity or non-dichotomy between humans and their natural environment, or, in the words of French social psychologist and environmental pioneer Serge Moscovici, the fact that "almost all of the natural world is now human while humans have always been natural."

Finally, I try to show throughout the book how metrics can change policy. Well-being and sustainability indicators now need to become performative and not just descriptive. While we should be concerned about obsessive quantification, blind monetization, and hazardous commodification, building, disseminating, and using alternative indicators is a practical way to reclaim essential values and advance important issues. Done properly, measuring produces positive social meaning. But we should not shy away from the ethical questions posed by valuation: Can we measure everything? Should we?

In short, this book is a critical exposé of well-being, resilience, and sustainability indicators, aimed at showing the interdependencies of their various dimensions in order to help change policy so as to advance the well-being and sustainability transition. Part I (chapters 1 and 2) sets the scene of our empirical world and affirms the need to govern our data-driven societies through the deconstruction of the dominance of standard economic metrics, chief among them GDP. It draws on the example of the European Union as a continent under the influence of powerful but flawed indicators.

Part II is organized to mirror a gradual understanding of the complexity of human well-being, from core economic well-being to the frontiers of sustainability analysis. It departs from the most familiar standard economic indicators to show how common notions such as personal income (chapter 3) or work (chapter 4) point to horizons that radically differ from gross domestic product growth. Chapters 5 through 7 enlarge the understanding of well-being to include human development indicators, both objective and subjective. Chapters 8 and 9 further widen the focal lens in order to make room for trust and institutions, thus moving from individual to collective well-being. Human well-being is then projected in time in order to identify the ecological conditions necessary for its perpetuation and highlight the social underpinning of sustainability. Chapter 10 shows how the economic sphere is contained in the biosphere and interacts with it (analysis of material flows), while chapter 11 demonstrates how unbalanced those exchanges have become, with the risk of short-term well-being destroying entire parts of the biosphere. Chapter 12 relates collective human development to the preservation of ecosystems (environmental performance indicators) and chapter 13 presents sustainability instruments and indicators that take the reader to the frontier of current knowledge, where as-yet unfinished metrics are being built in order to link well-being and sustainability. This organization reflects that the belief that we need to move beyond GDP is not so much a single composite indicator (replacing GDP with a counter-GDP) as policy area–specific indicators that form the building blocks of well-being and sustainability. We should not be looking so much for what Robert Costanza and his colleagues have called "the successor of GDP" as for its alternatives.[15] This pluralistic approach appears to be the best way to desacralize gross domestic product, not just in terms of substance, but also form.

Finally, part III (chapters 14 through 16) attempts to show how building good and resilient institutions at different levels of governance is the key to achieving the well-being and sustainability transition.

This book is an invitation to explore and understand our new economic world, where the passion for growth is gradually disappearing to make way for the pursuit of well-being (human flourishing), resilience (resistance to shocks), and sustainability (caring about the future). Because these three horizons have been overlooked by mainstream economics in the last three decades, our social world has been mismanaged and our prosperity is now threatened by inequality and ecological crises. Understanding how what matters to humans can be properly accounted for is the first step to valuing and taking care of what really counts.

PART I

The New Empirical Order

How Indicators (Mis)rule Our Economic World

The social power of numbers can be traced back to the philosophical tradition of Pythagoras and his disciples. They saw these digits as the secret codes of the physical universe and endowed them with moral values, giving them authority, if not agency, in the human world. For instance, the "golden ratio" (1.6180339887 . . .), one of the most famous numbers, first appeared in the writings of Euclid, but was renamed the "divine proportion" in Luca Pacioli's *De divina proportione* (1509), giving it a mystical dimension that persists until this day. Numbers have thus been seen for ages as keys to deciphering both the universe and the human mind. As they became instruments of knowledge embedded in modern mathematics and physics, they simultaneously became tools of political power and social control.

The power of what we today call data is indeed intimately related to the emergence of the nation-state, an institution of the modern era that used accounting to establish its sovereignty. Measuring people and available resources was intended, in the words of Adam Smith, to "first . . . supply a plentiful revenue or subsistence for the people . . . and secondly . . . supply the state or commonwealth with a revenue sufficient for the public services."[1] The science of statistics was born as accounting by the state, of the state, and for the state (which the German radical *Staat* clearly indicated), and was originally conceived to make war financially viable. William Petty in 1665 and then Gregory King in 1695 designed the first estimates of national income in England to allow the king to know how to pay for his warmongering. They were followed, in France, by Boisguilbert in 1697 and then Vauban in 1707, with the same motives.

It was the Belgian statistician Adolphe Quetelet, applying probability analysis to human behaviors (using averages and distribution), who turned sovereign accounting into social statistics by paying attention not just to the size or quantity of population but also to its quality, starting with health. (Quetelet invented the body mass index in 1832.) After the Second World War, with the expansion of the economic and social sphere in state activity, harmonized and ever-more-complex systems of national accounting were developed. Today, data are everywhere in public action. States govern with numbers as much as they are governed by them.

CHAPTER 1

The Ascent of "Datanomics"

The Case of the European Union

No region of the world embodies better the emergence of data-driven societies than one of its most recent political organizations: the European Union (EU). The European Community (which became the EU in 1992) was founded in 1957, based—with good reason—on the mistrust of politics. Rereading French foreign minister Robert Schuman's declaration of May 9, 1950, there is little doubt that this EU founding father saw unabashed political power as a threat to peace. In his eyes, it was necessary to deprive European countries of the means to destroy their fragile postwar peace, even if this meant that democracy had to be constrained. The constraint in question came in the form of economic rules[1] embedded in the Treaty of Rome (1957), which morphed with the Maastricht Treaty (1992) into quantitative criteria used to constantly monitor and evaluate member states from the moment of their admission into the various circles of European integration.[2]

The EU is today largely governed by numbers. The Maastricht Treaty is the economic constitution of contemporary Europe[3] and in it the political power of data is very tangible: ratios govern the admission of countries into the EU and the euro area and are supposed to guarantee the continent's stability, unity, and prosperity. Countries wanting to join the euro area when it was devised in the early 1990s had to conform to five criteria of convergence, three of which still govern the region's cohesion: inflation of no more than 1.5 percentage points above the average rate of the three EU member states with the lowest inflation over the previous year; a national budget deficit at or below 3 percent of gross domestic product; and national public debt not exceeding 60 percent of GDP. These rules have been only marginally modified in the past two decades. The European Central Bank (ECB) was assigned an inflation target of below but close to 2 percent when it was created in 1998. The Stability Pact governing fiscal policy includes a sanction procedure for "excessive" deficits and debt—over 3 percent and 60 percent of GDP, respectively—and forces governments to commit themselves to reaching "the medium-term objective of a budgetary position close to balance or in surplus."[4]

This project is officially motivated by the goal of paving the way for a better common future for European peoples, but the Stability Pact and the ECB statutes give priority to "price stability" and "fiscal sustainability," even if this means reducing governments' ability to deliver economic dynamism and employment expansion. Some indicators have been given prevalence over others out of political choice. But it is more and more clear that the intermediate objectives that prevail (fiscal balance, currency strength, price stability) are at odds in practice with the attainment of the ultimate social objectives (such as employment) that matter the most to populations.[5]

Countries belonging to the euro area, the most integrated part of the European project, have relied on these economic rules to govern their common policies. It can be said that the regulations have not served them well. If they have brought about an apparent culture of discipline, they were not able to create a lasting culture of cooperation: the "great recession" of 2008–2009 triggered a crisis that has, in recent years, turned into a lack of political trust among European citizens.[6] While economic discipline through numbers was supposed to ease peacetime relations, it has instead created divergence among nations and conflicts within their borders.

The early twenty-first century is emblematic in this regard. To date, European countries have been unable to cooperate in an effective and timely manner to build a coherent economic response to the 2008 crisis, straining their monetary union to the point where dissolution became an option. Without the intervention of the ECB, which has implicitly rewritten the European economic constitution and managed to salvage the euro in the summer of 2012 by overreaching its mandate,

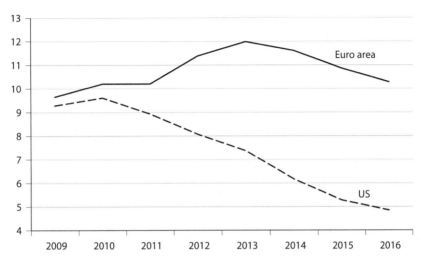

FIGURE 1.1. Unemployment rate, in % of total labor force. *Source*: IMF.

the European single currency might have imploded. The lack of resolve in 2008–2009 and the return to the enshrined reflex of restrictive austerity policies in 2010–2011 and onward has, in turn, further worsened social conditions in the EU and fueled political distrust.

The evolution of pre- and post-crisis unemployment rates is one possible illustration of the difference between a society governed by pragmatic economic policy and one governed by rigid economic rules. (See figure 1.1.) Both the euro area and the United States started with an almost identical rate in 2009. By 2016, unemployment in the former was twice as high as that in the latter.[7]

These contrasted outcomes, directly related to different policy responses, are anything but coincidental: they are determined by the respective economic constitutions of the United States and the European Union. While the Federal Reserve's core mission is to "conduct the nation's monetary policy by influencing the monetary and credit conditions in the economy in pursuit of maximum employment, stable prices, and moderate long-term interest rates," the ECB must first and foremost "maintain price stability," which is narrowly defined as "a year-on-year increase in the Harmonized Index of Consumer Prices (HICP) for the euro area of below 2 percent." This difference explains why, in the face of the first signs of recession in 2008, the ECB increased its interest rate, compounding the shock instead of buffering it, while the Fed had already started to decrease its policy rate. As we have seen, the same kind of constraint weighs on fiscal policy and explains why the euro area imposed a negative fiscal shock on its ailing economy while the United States was putting in place the largest fiscal stimulus of its history. Because of the power some indicators have acquired on European economic policy, the culture of discipline has stifled the culture of cooperation and Europeans have paid a high price for it.

Of course, certain countries, most notably Germany, have been able to restore some collective protections that have alleviated the ultimate social impact of the macroeconomic shock, but most EU member states were severely hurt by the 2009 recession, which has actually shaken and damaged the very core of European integration. What is more, it also resulted in an increase of support for populist parties openly hostile to European integration, a support that was clearly visible with the European elections of May 2014[8] and continues to upset political systems all through Europe, as it did in June 2016 when British citizens decided to exit from the European Union. The current wave of European populism is a direct consequence of the distrust toward European integration.

In a context of economic insecurity and identity anxiety, populism is indeed becoming a widespread feature of the European political landscape. From France to Italy, Norway to Greece, Finland to the United Kingdom, populism is not only making direct political gains but also influencing moderate parties in power through agenda-setting on immigration and security. France is a case in point, with right-wing President Nicolas Sarkozy (2007 to 2012) and then left-wing Prime Minister Manuel Valls (2014 to 2016) embracing part of the far-right political agenda on nationality reform and law-and-order policy.

This political crisis has a lot to do with the "automatic pilot" mode dictated by the inscription of economic rules in the EU's fundamental texts. In such a pseudo-federal system, political deliberation should be about how to finance and produce the public goods that benefit all European citizens, not respecting abstract ratios regardless of real economic conditions. Those European public goods are far more important to the welfare of European citizens than the scrupulous observance of doctrinal criteria of budgetary and monetary stability, which, at their best, constitute intermediary objectives for economic policy and, at their worse, prevent the final objectives from being reached (as when inflation is given preference over employment). It is true that member states retain a great deal of power in the EU, more power, in fact, than either the European Commission or the European Parliament have today. But their political bargaining power is bound by the EU Treaties and their quantified commitments.

There is a real European paradox regarding economic indicators since the great recession: on the one hand, the EU has tried to capitalize on the discontent with standard economics and to embrace the "beyond GDP" agenda; on the other, it has become even more rigid in applying its ill-advised targets. The communication "GDP and Beyond: Measuring Progress in a Changing World," released in 2009 by the European Commission, described ways to improve indicators in order to better reflect societal concerns. The commission's intent was to adjust and complement GDP with indicators that monitored social and environmental progress.[9] Yet, so far, the new strategy has not produced tangible results in changing European governance, which still relies heavily on conventional economic indicators. What is more, while the European Union was putting forward these new indicators, it was also coercing the Greek government, from 2010 onward, into reaching European ratios in a time of recession, delaying the country's economic recovery by several years, imposing extremely difficult social conditions on the Greek population,[10] and creating perilous political tensions among member states.[11]

As the European example makes clear, democracy ends up at risk when too much confidence is put by policy makers on too-narrow indicators. We now need to define simple but robust criteria of good and bad economic indicators (and their usage). These will help us to understand why GDP is fast losing its relevance in the twenty-first century.

CHAPTER 2

Good and Bad Indicators

The Case of GDP

How can we know with a fair degree of certainty that governing twenty-first-century economies with conventional economic indicators such as GDP is a bad idea? We first need to learn more about the qualities and flaws of various economic indicators. An indicator is a simplified representation of a complex social reality. It can serve as both a policy input and a policy outcome. It can aid in the design or the evaluation of a given policy, or both.[1] It is used to perform three main tasks: to know and understand, to administer and govern, and to communicate and represent. An indicator should thus possess three fundamental attributes: formal quality, policy purpose, and political impact.

As for its formal qualities, a good indicator must be accurate, timely, regular, comparable in time and space, disaggregative (that is, it should have a certain granularity), and evolutive, to allow for improvements. But it also needs substantive qualities. A good indicator should be purposeful (that is, measure precisely what it was designed for), policy-relevant, to inform on the real complexity of the social world, and socially appropriable, which is to say, both understandable by citizens and subject to public debate.

Obviously, there are trade-offs between these qualities: purposefulness often contradicts availability, appropriability can hinder formal qualities, and regularity can pose a problem for relevance. Two major types of policy indicators offer a glimpse of ways to deal with these dilemmas. Composite or synthetic indicators offer a one-dimensional

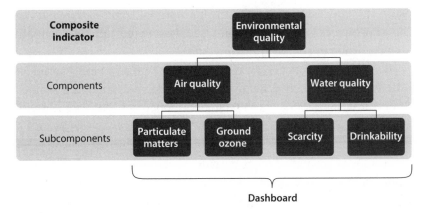

FIGURE 2.1. Composite indicators and dashboards: a simple example.

view of the social world: they are easily readable and understandable and are comparable in time and space. However, they inevitably bring about issues of data aggregation and weighting, both of which relate to the need to combine heterogeneous variables such as income (expressed in monetary units) and health (expressed in years of life expectancy) in a single piece of information. This is by no means technically impossible, but necessitates the use of specific statistical techniques.[2] The second of these policy indicators, the dashboard, allows the user the freedom not to choose between these different dimensions by adopting a multidimensional approach, which retains the maximum possible amount of information for action. Assessing environmental quality, for example, might mean quantifying air quality, water quality, climate, and other dimensions that are not akin to one another. This, in turn, brings about other problems such as data heterogeneity, hierarchy, and comparability in time and ranking in space.

There is, however, less contradiction between composite indicators and dashboards than is often understood. Figure 2.1 shows how dashboards can be conceived as a step in building a composite indicator. In this theoretical example, an environmental quality indicator is designed with only two dimensions, air quality and water quality, themselves aggregating two subdimensions. The key issue in the choice between a composite indicator and a dashboard is the possibility and relevance of aggregation of the subcomponents, as statistical information is being lost in this process and dimensions become reducible to one another. Choosing between a dashboard and a composite indicator is essentially knowing when to stop aggregating data.

This issue is one of the many raised by the gross domestic product, or GDP. From a technical standpoint, GDP can be defined as a composite indicator measuring marketable and monetized economic activity. It uses monetization of its components' value at their market price and imputation of the value of those not sold on markets to aggregate many dimensions of economic activity, some positive (nutrition, health, education, environmental protection), others less so (arms expenditures or prisons, items sometimes referred to as "regrettables"). By conflating positive and negative elements, GDP not only muddles the social picture, but hides from policy view important evolutions in well-being and sustainability by giving the illusion that each of its components is in a good place because its aggregated sum is growing. GDP is thus often confused with well-being and even sustainability, while in reality it says very little, if anything, of either.

The context in which indicators are born is often an indicator itself of their strengths and weaknesses. GDP was first developed in 1934 by Simon Kuznets at the demand of the US Congress, whose members wanted to have a clear and synthetic view of what had happened to the American economy after the 1929 stock market crash. What had happened was the Great Depression. The prehistorical GDP built by Kuznets had the great merit of showing the huge contraction of almost all sectors of the American economy in the first years of the 1930s. Because the shock was systemic, a synthetic indicator was fully relevant and called for a systemic macroeconomic response, something President Roosevelt eventually achieved with the New Deal and the war effort.

Putting the first insights of the nascent pre-Keynesian macroeconomic discipline to good use, Kuznets offered three simple ways to calculate GDP, each time relying on the monetary value of goods and services produced in the country over a given period. The first was through the production approach: the aggregation of the added value of all monetized economic activities in a year. The second, equivalent measure was through the aggregation of all income distributed in the economy (i.e., profits + wages − taxes), and the third, the sum of all expenditures in the economy (summing all the components of demand). Although Kuznets invented the process, he did not invent its name: it was Clark Warburton who first used in print the term "gross national product," which Kuznets later adopted.

Therefore, interestingly, GDP was not born as an indicator of development but as a symptom of crisis. Even more telling, Kuznets was keenly aware that GDP relied on debatable methodological choices, writing, "The national income total is thus an amalgam of relatively accurate and only approximate estimates rather than a unique, highly precise measurement."[3] Going further, Kuznets warned of the "uses and abuses of national income measurements":

> The valuable capacity of the human mind to simplify a complex situation in a compact characterization becomes dangerous when not controlled in terms of definitely stated criteria. With quantitative measurements especially, the definiteness of the result suggests, often misleadingly, a precision and simplicity in the outlines of the object measured. Measurements of national income are subject to this type of illusion and resulting abuse, especially since they deal with matters that are the center of conflict of opposing social groups where the effectiveness of an argument is often contingent upon oversimplification . . .[4]

He was rightly cautious. The so-called Kuznets curve, an abusive generalization of his 1955 article observing the U-inverted relation between growth and inequality in certain countries at a specific historical juncture, was interpreted by many economists as implying that increasing GDP per capita would mechanically reduce inequality and could even lead to solutions for environmental crises. (The "environmental Kuznets curve" posits that, past a certain income per capita threshold, environmental degradations gently recede.)

GDP, its own inventor warned us, is not an indicator of well-being or sustainability. Yet it became endowed with not only the magical power to solve inequality crises, but also to mitigate environmental ones, which to this day remains an enduring belief in economic circles.

The second key moment setting the stage for the reign of GDP was the 1944 conference convened among the Allied nations in Bretton Woods, New Hampshire, when the new international economic order came to life under the leadership of the United States. Another moment of crisis gave birth to the first effort to harmonize national accounting: how national resources should be used to pay for war—the very question that gave birth to the first attempts to build national accounts by Petty and King in the seventeenth century—triggered new research in the UK. James Meade and Richard Stone, associates of John Maynard Keynes, the founding father of macroeconomic analysis, gave life to GDP as we know it.[5]

At Bretton Woods, GDP became the currency of national success, the sign that a country belonged among the most advanced in the world. From then on, a nation would be considered "developed" if its GDP per capita was as high as that of the richest countries. The decades that followed were marked by the imperative of reconstruction in many countries and by the need to advance the material conditions of people in the race between the "free world" and the other winner of 1945, the USSR. Industrial growth was logically put at the center of increasingly harmonized national accounts. Social progress meant growth and growth meant industrial growth. For the first time, national accounting was used to pursue a new quest other than war and to ask an entirely new question: how to pay for development.

Why and how did GDP become gradually irrelevant? Using the criteria defined at the beginning of this chapter, it can be said that its formal qualities have greatly improved and are possibly stronger than ever, but that its substantive qualities are probably weaker than at any other time. This weakness is reinforced by its misuse to evaluate and represent realities it was never meant to measure. To take a simple example, GDP still does a good job of detecting and tracking economic recessions, but it cannot measure their social impact. When good indicators are poorly used, they become bad ones.

Ironically, the great strength of GDP is now its most critical flaw. Macroeconomic reasoning is fundamentally correct in highlighting the interdependence of economic actors and the impact of their interaction beyond individual (or microeconomic) behaviors. This well-established stream of economic theory was overlooked by the governments that engaged in austerity in the face of the "great recession."[6] But it turns out that the circle is even wider, well beyond GDP's remit, for beyond economic well-being stand human well-being and, even more importantly, sustainable human well-being.

Because the crisis of GDP is substantial rather than just formal, the various attempts to build "1.1" and "2.0" versions in order to make it relevant again, while well-intentioned and valuable, fell short of meeting the challenges of the twenty-first century. "GDP 1.1" promoters now recognize that gross domestic product only reflects market and monetary exchanges considered in the too-narrow limits of national borders without accounting for the depreciation of productive structures (capital). GDP's "gross" nature has led to the development of Net National Income, which attempts to take into account capital depreciation,[7] while its "domestic" limit encouraged the use of GNP as an alternative to GDP.[8] "GDP 2.0" is attempting something even more ambitious. It is trying to take stock of the considerable evolution of our postwar economic world and to include international trade (especially complex financial flows and the global supply chain) and the price and quality of intangible goods and services such as knowledge in national accounts innovation.[9] Growth might thus be better measured through GDP 1.1 and GDP 2.0, but the stakes are actually higher: it is our passion for (GDP) growth that should be questioned, not just its measurement.

GDP's relevance is fast declining in the beginning of the twenty-first century, alongside that of the other conventional economic indicators of which it is the flagship. Economic growth, so buoyant during the three decades following the Second World War, has gradually faded away in advanced and even developing economies and is therefore becoming an ever-more-elusive goal for policy. Both objective and subjective well-being—those things that make life worth living—are visibly more and more disconnected from economic growth, as this book will make clear. GDP also tells us all but nothing about sustainability, the compatibility of our current well-being with the long-term viability of ecosystems, even though it is clearly the major challenge we and our descendants must face.

To put it simply, what we need to understand is not whether growth will be strong or weak in the coming years, but that the return of strong growth would ensure neither that individual well-being would improve nor that societies would become more sustainable. We thus need to work in three new directions in order to really understand our economic world.

The area I call "below GDP" includes the fundamental determinants of human development. These explain the quantitative accumulation of production factors and the qualitative improvement of their combination that are necessary for production and per-capita incomes to rise. For centuries institutions, geography, and international openness have been combined in various ways under all latitudes to enlarge or restrict the range of human development opportunities. Economic development depends on these deep determinants; attention should therefore be focused on them, rather than on a superficial dimension such as "growth."

The factors "beside GDP" are the nonmonetary things that benefit or hinder human well-being, such as health and education. They cannot be subsumed to income. The idea that economic growth represents development, insofar as it would be a satisfactory summary measure of all dimensions of human well-being, is simply wrong. GDP growth is not another term for human development; in fact, it is often its antonym. Hence, increasing the former will not, on its own, improve the latter: specific policies are needed that directly target education, health, environmental conditions, or democratic quality. For lack of consideration of this plurality of well-being, a single dimension, usually the economic one, will dominate all the others and crush them, mutilating human development in the process.

The "beyond GDP" category highlights the ecological challenge: Does a 10 percent GDP growth rate matter if the ecosystems, water, and air that underpin our well-being are being devastated over a span of two or three decades? Is economic growth worth anything if life itself becomes impossible? To use the words of Chinese Environment Minister Zhou Shengxian in 2011, "If our planet is wrecked and our health ravaged, what is the benefit of our development?"[10] Our economic and political systems exist only within a larger context, the biosphere, whose vitality is the source of their survival and perpetuation. If ecological crises are not measured, monitored, and mitigated, they will eventually wipe out human well-being.

PART II

Mapping and Measuring Well-Being and Sustainability in the Twenty-First Century

How can we measure what really matters? Let's start by mapping it. In this part, we start with economic well-being, then move toward the frontier of current research in sustainability analysis and measurement. The overall framework reflecting our progression from dimension to dimension and chapter to chapter is represented in figure II.1. Chapters 3 and 4 (respectively income and work, which stand for economic well-being) are at the center of the figure, while chapter 13 brings the reader to the last, outer circle, sustainable well-being.

This figure has three essential meanings. The first, which is obvious, is that GDP measures only a tiny fraction of the complexity of modern human societies. It measures some but not all economic well-being, does not account for the other dimensions of well-being, and does not account for sustainability. As we will see in the next few chapters, it is already disqualified as an accurate analysis and policy instrument, even for simple economic well-being dimensions such as income and

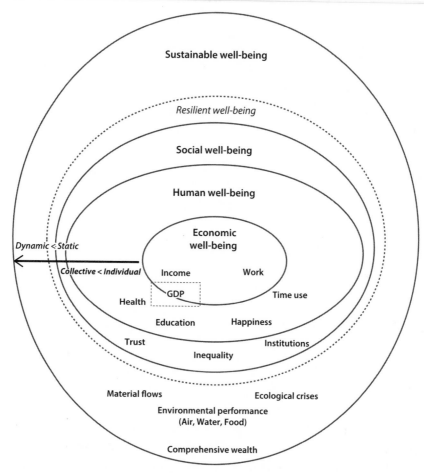

FIGURE II.1. Mapping and measuring well-being, resilience, and sustainability.

work. What is more, while GDP partially measures some human development dimensions (e.g., health, education), it does so based on their supply cost and not their outcomes or the actual benefits they provide (health status, educational attainments). As we will see in the corresponding chapters, the quality of a health or education system, especially in developed countries, cannot be properly assessed by its overall cost, although GDP can be a useful benchmark indicator to assess the magnitude of national education expenditures. These well-being dimensions have an obvious relation to the most influential theories of human welfare and justice. Primary goods, as imagined by John Rawls, include the basic rights and liberties, freedom of movement, and free choice among a wide range of occupations, the powers of offices and positions of responsibility, income and wealth, and the social bases of self-respect.[1] Capabilities, as envisioned by Amartya Sen and Martha Nussbaum, include life, bodily health, bodily integrity, senses, imagination and thought, emotions, practical reason, affiliation, other species, play, and control over one's environment. People act out most capabilities through functions such as education, health, and income.[2]

The second meaning of this framework is that the well-being dimensions are cumulative: We can choose to look at (and take care of) only economic well-being or capture human well-being and social well-being as well. (The latter case means embracing not just an individual approach to well-being, but a collective one also, by, for instance, measuring the quality of institutions such as a judiciary system or parliament.) Then we can choose to further enlarge our concern and add a time component to our analysis by trying to measure whether our interactions with the biosphere can be sustained tomorrow and the day after without damaging our well-being. By doing so, we move from a static approach of well-being to a dynamic one. But why should we care about the quality of education, the reduction of inequality, or the depletion of trust if indicators related to ecological crises reveal to us that we are on the verge of a near-collapse of the biosphere? What is the point of reworking education systems to achieve more equality if whole human habitats will disintegrate within a few decades?

This is where the third meaning comes in. This framework represents an attempt to link together well-being, resilience, and sustainability to understand their synergies. Well-being without sustainability, or resilience understood as short-term sustainability, are just illusions. Our planet's climate crisis has the potential to destroy the unprecedented contemporary progress in human health in a mere few decades. If China's ecosystems collapse under the weight of hypergrowth, with no unpolluted water left to drink nor clean air to breathe, the hundreds of millions of people in that country who have escaped poverty since the 1980s will be thrown back into it and worse. If the outer circles in figure II.1 collapse, then the inner ones will follow suit, while the opposite is not true. The mention of "air, water, and food" along with environmental performance means that the outer circle contains vital well-being. But sustainability without well-being is just an ideal. Human behaviors and attitudes will become more sustainable not to "save the planet," but to preserve well-being. What is more, as argued convincingly by the late Elinor Ostrom, social cooperation is the key to sustainable practices and social cooperation depends critically on education, equality, trust, and good institutions (which are to be found in the figure's inner circles).[3] Comprehensive wealth, the ultimate metric representing sustainable well-being, means both that well-being is approached in a multidimensional way and tracked through time in a dynamic manner.

The 2009 Stiglitz Commission recommended that a distinction be made "between an assessment of current well-being and an assessment of sustainability."[4] But the commission, which was focused on measurement issues, also urged that "measures of well-being . . . be put in a context of sustainability." In other words, while well-being and sustainability should not be confused or conflated in a single metric, neither should they be separated analytically: they should, on the contrary, both be articulated.

This well-being/sustainability nexus (how well-being can serve sustainability, and sustainability serve well-being), brilliantly captured by Partha Dasgupta in his seminal work, cannot be overstated.[5] One amusing way to articulate the fundamental conundrum it represents is to go back to the dry but profound humor of Groucho Marx, who once complained, "Why should I care about future generations? What have they ever done for me?" This is the key question. How can we make taking care of those we will never know desirable? How can we transform our preoccupation with the future into present well-being? The only way is to link the well-being of future generations to the well-being of the current ones. This is precisely how devising and using sustainability indicators instead of GDP and growth helps. For instance, when China reduces GDP growth and its use of coal, local and global pollution decreases. By taking care of future generations, the current generations take care of themselves.

The following chapters will ask the same few questions regarding a given indicator for each dimension of well-being and sustainability: How does it change our vision of the economic world when compared

to a standard one such as GDP and income? What is the policy consequence that can result from it? What recommendations for policy makers does the indicator entail? What are its limitations?

The approach to well-being in this book is both pluralistic and dynamic. It attempts to highlight the plurality of well-being (showing
how each dimension differs from growth) and demonstrate how those
building blocks can be combined to guide policy beyond GDP.

CHAPTER 3

Income

Personal income is a good introduction to exploring the complexity of human well-being: it is at the core of economic well-being, yet is strikingly disconnected from its most widely used measures and those of GDP and its by-products, growth and GDP per capita. Indeed, considering individual or household income rather than growth allows us to explore the difference between production and consumption, the latter of which is made possible by income. More importantly, it lets us distinguish between production and the effective distribution of the fruits of the production effort among different members of society. Measuring income rather than GDP alone hence enables us to grasp one of the most fundamental economic evolutions of the past three decades: the crisis of inequality. It also helps us distinguish two fundamental well-being measurement issues that were raised by Amartya Sen in his seminal study of poverty and famines: the question of identification (what constitutes well-being at the individual level) and that of aggregation (how the distribution of a given well-being dimension such as income is accounted for at the social level).

Simon Kuznets, the inventor of GDP, was well aware of the importance of distribution patterns in the proper assessment of welfare. He wrote in 1934 that "Economic welfare cannot be adequately measured unless the personal distribution of income is known" and that "The welfare of a nation can, therefore, scarcely be inferred from a measurement of national income."[1] But this warning has largely been ignored with the widespread postwar use of GDP and the ever-narrowing focus of economics on efficiency to the detriment of equity. At three critical moments, distributional economics gave way to a productivity-focused economics largely blind to inequality. The foundation of the American Economic Association coincided with the intellectual ascension of Charles F. Dunbar (and the retreat of Richard T. Ely), who viewed economics as a science that should stay clear of ethical considerations. The development of welfare theorems by Léon Walras in 1920 and Vilfredo Pareto in 1930 conflated productive and distributional issues. Finally, the "great dilemma" posited by Arthur Okun between equity and efficiency in the 1970s—the former being assimilated as a loss in terms of the latter—separated even more mainstream economics from distributional concerns.

Yet, distributional economics has made a remarkable comeback in the past decade. This new focus is not a conceptual breakthrough, but rather a return to pre–twentieth century economics, a return that was anticipated in the 1970s and 1980s by two precursors. The first was Amartya Sen, who challenged economic rationality and re-embedded economic activity in ideas of justice; the second was Anthony Atkinson, who developed pioneering empirical work on the measurement of inequality.

Contemporary studies show that inequality is not only unjust, but also inefficient. Consequently, an economic policy that would not pay enough attention to this dimension of human well-being would be perilous even from the strict efficiency point of view. Inequality can cause financial crises and tends to replace innovation with rent.[2] It hinders health and education.[3] It paralyzes democracy.[4] And it exacerbates environmental degradation and feeds ecological crises.[5]

To understand how income indicators can help us explore the true complexity of our economic world beyond GDP and point us toward relevant policy, we need to start with elementary definitions. Measuring personal income generally means measuring "household income," the income that actually reaches households at the end of the process of economic income creation and distribution. The great distribution of income, also called functional distribution, begins between wages and profits (that is, between firms and individuals). For instance, the share of wages in the added value created by the French economy declined from 75 to about 60 percent between the early 1980s and the late 2000s. Similar changes can be observed in other Organisation for Economic Co-operation and Development (OECD) countries over the same period of time. Once this first distinction has been made, we can further refine the picture by measuring the share of overall profits going to the financial sector, represented by the distribution of dividends by companies to their shareholders. To continue with the example of France, this share was on the order of 30 percent in the early 1980s and rose to nearly 80 percent in the early 2010s.

Using these two simple indicators of income distribution, one can thus highlight two major developments that many advanced economies have shared over the past three decades: the marked decline of labor's share in the overall added value or profits and the acute financialization of the economy. Even the most careful study of GDP and its growth over this period cannot shed light on any of these dynamics. After profits and dividends have been taken into account, inequality between households will be the final determinant of personal income distribution—or, to use the lay term, who gets what.

There are thus two ways to escape the misrepresentations of GDP when it comes to assessing people's income. The first is to "deflate" GDP growth from finance and focus on the industrial sector to account for economic dynamism or the lack thereof; the second is to deflate growth from inequality by focusing on median income or building distributional rather than national (production) accounts.

But is there really a stark difference between the measurement of economic development by GDP, corporate profits, and financial markets on the one hand and household income on the other? Can we not say that these metrics, without being completely identical, at least move in the same direction? The answer is no. A detour via recent US data makes this point very clearly.

When household income rather than GDP per capita growth is considered as an indicator of economic well-being of Americans in recent times, we learn that the "economic recovery" that many commentators have been trumpeting since 2010, based on production, profits, and stock-market data, is simply not a reality for the vast majority of households in the United States. A simple alternative indicator that can be used here is the median household income, which divides the population between the 50 percent earning more and the 50 percent earning less. (This was close to $53,650 per year in 2014.) This is a much more relevant way to measure household income than just dividing GDP by the number of inhabitants. This GDP per head or per capita assumes that each "head" receives the same income. (A well-known joke has it that when Bill Gates walks into a bar, everyone becomes a millionaire "on average.")

Available data exhibit two clear trends during the phase of GDP recovery (from 2010 onwards): a decline in median household income and an increase in income inequality among households. The first phenomenon goes well beyond the current period: some calculations show that, while GDP increased by 260 percent in the United States between 1967 and 2013, from \$4.65 trillion to \$16.77 trillion, in real terms, median household income increased by only 19 percent, from \$43,558 to \$51,939.[6] When compared term to term, GDP per capita more than doubled during the period, while median income per capita increased by only 17 percent. This suggests that a substantial amount of income has been created in the US economy in the last fifty years, but not distributed to households.

On the second point, French economist Emmanuel Saez of the University of California, Berkeley, has shown that, while GDP growth was, in fact, resuming between 2009 and 2012, 90 percent of the income gains during this period were actually captured by the top 1 percent of income distribution. In other words, the "recovery" was a mirage for 99 percent of US citizens, who saw their income grow on average by only 0.8 percent between 2009 and 2012 while the income of the richest 1 percent increased by about 35 percent in the same time (or forty-five times more).

GDP tells us nothing about these inequality dynamics and yet they are absolutely essential to understanding not only economics but also politics. The popularity of former President Barack Obama's economic policy, measured by citizen approval ratings, has followed the evolution of median household income and not that of GDP. Gallup's data make it possible to see that, while US GDP was recovering from the year 2010, the economic unpopularity of Barack Obama followed the curve of median household income (figures 3.1 and 3.2). The disconnect between the reality experienced by US households and the optimistic discourse of the president on the state of the economy based on GDP growth explains in part the strongly Republican outcome of the

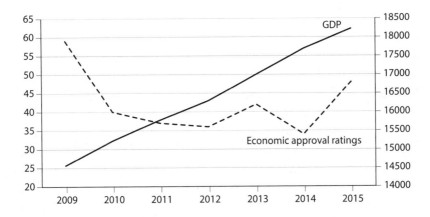

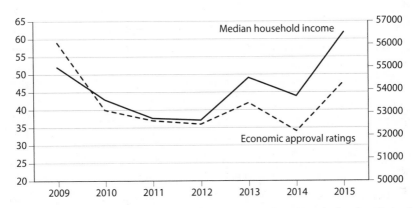

FIGURES 3.1 AND 3.2. GDP, income, and economic approvals in the United States (2009–2015). GDP is in billions of dollars and median household income in thousands of dollars; economic approval ratings measure the percentage of Americans who say they approve of the way the president is handling the economy. *Source*: Gallup and BEA.

midterm elections of 2014. The conclusion is clear: betting on GDP can make you lose an election!

This gap between GDP per capita and household income is not unique to the United States. OECD countries during the worst of the "great recession" experienced large differences between the two, with GDP per capita exceeding household income in 85 percent of countries.

On average, the gap reached almost 1.8 percentage points, equivalent to a strong recession. In the case of Greece and Iceland, the difference was considerably higher. This means that in 85 percent of the most developed economies, household income growth was almost 2 percentage points below GDP per capita growth at a critical economic time, blurring policy makers' vision of the situation.[7] Those countries' reliance on GDP made it effectively impossible to understand what households were actually experiencing.

International comparisons on the basis of income rather than GDP are, by contrast, very enlightening. The consideration given not only to the overall wealth of a country as measured by GDP, but to the actual distribution of income among its citizens, can lead to rethinking the vision we have of the hierarchy of nations. Data recently compiled by the Luxembourg Income Study on median per capita disposable income (income available after taxes and social transfers) show a striking reality: if the American middle class has been the richest in the world since the 1980s, it was joined in 2010 by the Canadian middle class and is now closely followed by those of Norway and the Netherlands, due to the wage stagnation of the majority of the US population and the much more effective redistribution occurring in some Western countries.[8]

By the same token, when inequality indicators are refined using real average income rather than average GDP per capita and comparing only the bottom 90 percent of the income distribution, the United States falls behind not just Canada but most of the developed countries. As shown in the 2015 Economic Report of the President by economists working for the Council of Economic Advisers, growth of real average income for the least rich 90 percent of the population put the United States behind Canada, the United Kingdom, France, Italy, Germany, and Japan as early as 1970 and up until today.[9] There is thus a need for a new indicator summing up national accounts not just in terms of production but also distribution. This is precisely what the still-experimental "distributional national account," or DNA, seeks to do, combining tax surveys and national accounts data to build new data series on the distribution of national income, beginning with the United States.[10]

Exploring the relationship between income and economic policy further can provide us with yet more insights. Household income depends on three main components: income from commercial activities or "market income" (derived from work and the capital owned by individuals), taxes and contributions paid to public authorities, and social benefits received from those authorities. Household income therefore does not consist only of market income and should be properly measured as "gross disposable income," or market income from which relevant taxes are subtracted and to which any benefits received are added. This breakdown may seem a bit technical, but it is extremely valuable to understanding the mechanisms at work in the economic crisis triggered in 2009.

The OECD has carried out a breakdown of household income in the thirty-five richest countries of the world for the years 2007 to 2011 that shows that if market income fell by 1.3 percent on average each year during this period, the positive impact of taxation and social transfers cushioned the shock of the crisis by up to 0.9 percent annually, for an overall decline of only 0.4 percent per year of household income. In other words, tax and social systems divided by three the impact of the crisis for households living in OECD countries, a key fact that GDP growth could not capture.

This policy mechanism also helps us understand why austerity policy put in place in many European countries after 2010 was detrimental to household income. A breakdown of the income of French households between the years 2010 and 2013 shows a total loss of income of over €1,600, reflecting an average decline in market income of about €1,000, a rise in social benefits of €350, and a tax increase of about €950. Three effects are thus combined here: the economic crisis, which accounts for the loss in market income; the support of the welfare state, which partially offsets the decline in market income; and finally austerity policy—in this case, the increase of household taxation in order to meet European fiscal criteria—which led to cuts in household income almost as high as the economic crisis itself. The result was a significant drop in the income of French households even though GDP grew annually around 1.2 percent during the 2010–2013 period. This breakdown of income helps us understand both the positive impact of the welfare state and the negative impact of austerity policies that aggravated market mechanisms instead of correcting them. We can learn even more on the key question of redistribution with the proper indicators.

The Gini index measures the extent to which the distribution of income among individuals within an economy deviates from a perfectly equal distribution.[11] A Gini index of zero indicates perfect equality and 1, perfect inequality. More generally, the comparison of Gini indexes before and after taxes and transfers sheds very useful light on the magnitude of income inequality resulting from the distribution of monetary resources by markets and the subsequent redistribution of these resources by public authorities. Table 3.1 shows that the impact of redistribution in the OECD is quite strong: on average, taxes and transfers reduce the Gini index (the level of inequality) by more than 25 percent and, in some countries, such as Finland and Austria, by close to 65 percent.

What is more, we can learn a great deal from these data about the inequality profile of countries and the policy that could correct them. Some nations, such as France, display higher than average levels of market inequality but lower than average disposable income inequality, suggesting that the redistribution system is effective but also that inequality in health and education leads to important "primary" inequality that cannot be fully reduced by taxes and transfers. (Chapter 6 will confirm this diagnosis for France.) In the United States and the UK, however, inequality levels of market and disposable income appear closer to one another and rank both near the top of OECD countries.

Using the concept of "standard of living," often related to disposable income, we can make further progress in understanding the real situation of people in a time of economic crisis. The first very conventional new element to consider is inflation (price increases), which allows us to refine gross disposable income into "purchasing power." (GDI is deflated by prices and thus becomes net of inflation, reflecting the real consumption of goods and services available.) The year 2012 is particularly striking in terms of the evolution of living standards in France. According to the French statistical agency INSEE's data, inflation reached 1.4 percent that year, while gross disposable income grew by 0.9 percent, resulting in a decline of purchasing power of 0.5 percent. Thus in 2012, because of these developments, French households objectively saw their standard of living decline.

But a second, aggravating factor comes into play: a portion of household expenditures are called "preempted" because households must pay them each month before they can even think about how they are going to spend their income. This is particularly true of housing expenditure

TABLE 3.1. Inequality (Gini coefficient) of market income and disposable (net) income in the OECD area, working-age persons, late 2000s

	Gini coefficient of market income	Gini coefficient of disposable income	
South Korea	0.323	0.2296	Slovenia
Switzerland	0.338	0.2433	Denmark
Iceland	0.3457	0.2532	Czech Republic
Slovak Republic	0.3628	0.2534	Slovak Republic
Sweden	0.368	0.2561	Norway
Slovenia	0.3723	0.2563	Belgium
Denmark	0.3744	0.258	Finland
Norway	0.3764	0.2588	Sweden
Czech Republic	0.3804	0.2607	Austria
Estonia	0.3889	0.2902	Switzerland
Netherlands	0.3908	0.2915	Luxembourg
Japan	0.3916	0.292	France
Finland	0.403	0.2972	Netherlands
New Zealand	0.403	0.3	Germany
Spain	0.4052	0.3	Korea
Austria	0.4062	0.3005	Iceland
Belgium	0.4081	0.3056	Estonia
Canada	0.4158	0.3097	Poland
Australia	0.418	0.313	Spain
Germany	0.4197	0.323	New Zealand
France	0.431	0.3235	Japan
Poland	0.4348	0.3236	Australia
Luxembourg	0.4363	0.3283	Canada
United States	0.4527	0.3342	Italy
United Kingdom	0.4559	0.3446	United Kingdom
Portugal	0.4581	0.3467	Portugal
Italy	0.4647	0.3587	Israel
Israel	0.4648	0.3701	United States
Chile	0.5228	0.4961	Chile
OECD average	0.4073	0.3041	OECD average

Source: OECD.

(rent or mortgage)[12] and mobile and Internet subscriptions, which are often paid by direct debit. These expenditures represent, on average, 30 percent of the typical French budget (with strong inequalities according to income level), and their share has doubled in recent decades, mostly because of rising housing costs, which has been a factor in many other countries.

Once these expenditures are considered, the standard of living of French households in 2012 was even lower: it fell by 2.3 percent, while GDP growth showed an increase of 0.4 percent. In other words, there is almost a three-percentage-point difference between the state of the economy as portrayed by GDP and the economic situation experienced by households.

Once again, these breakdowns may seem technical, but the economic realities behind the statistics are perfectly understandable by ordinary people due to the simple fact that they experience them on a daily basis. Everyone knows what a preempted expenditure is, while no one has ever met GDP or "growth." From a policy maker perspective, relying on irrelevant indicators amounts to blinding oneself to the actual state of the economy and running the risk of speaking a foreign language to one's fellow citizens. Moreover, the various income indicators that we have briefly reviewed play a crucial role in guiding policy to the root causes of income stagnation (or rising income inequality between households).

However, despite these insights, it is still a challenge to arrive at a true understanding of "good" indicators of economic well-being. A 2011 American study shows that a considerable gap can exist among three variables: desired income, perceived, and observed income inequality.[13] When asked, US citizens are inclined toward better redistribution and would like 30 percent of revenues to go to the richest 20 percent of people and 10 percent to the poorest 20 percent. But they believe that 60 percent of income goes to the richest 20 percent and only 2 percent to the poorest 20 percent. In reality, 85 percent of US income is owned by the richest 20 percent of the population, while the remaining 80 percent of people share 15 percent of the total. (The poorest 20 percent hold a microscopic part, close to 0, of all income generated by the US economy.) This misunderstanding of the economic reality presents a major obstacle to reducing inequality; the first step toward fighting inequality, therefore, must be the dissemination of the correct economic facts so that citizens can support those public officials who share their preferences—in the case of this study, those politicians proposing tax reforms that would ensure redistribution of income closer to their own wishes.

As we have seen so far in this chapter, many different income indicators can be used to better understand the reality of economic well-being. But an even more fundamental issue is how income itself and its uneven distribution is determined. In other words, we should be interested not just in indicators that show the consequences of inequality (such as the inequality ratio between the richest and poorest citizens), but also in causal indicators: those factors that determine whether the gap between rich and poor is large or small. Research on this issue has made significant progress in recent years, so that we are now able to distinguish not only between the different components of income, but also between factors that determine these components, such as international trade, employment policies, family structures, and the effectiveness of the tax and benefit system. Together, these determinants define "inequality profiles" for national economies. They highlight the drivers for inequality in different countries and thereby point the way to formulating country-specific policies for inequality reduction.[14] But can we go even further and understand the dynamic of inequality, i.e., the evolution of inequality in time?

One of the key questions raised by the current crisis of income inequality in the United States and many countries of the developed and emerging world is the possibility that inequalities are reproduced from generation to generation, so that social inequality becomes a self-sustaining mechanism that policy is unable to stop. To understand this problem and the social perils of dynastic societies that gradually undermine democracy and the meritocratic principle, it is necessary to move from static to dynamic indicators. These can take two main forms. The first is the notion of wealth or assets, which reflects the stock of accumulated income over the years (the difference between a monthly salary and a savings account or investment portfolio). In this respect, wealth inequality data show an even more concerning situation for the US economy than income inequality, with the top 0.1 percent of the population now holding as much wealth as the bottom 90 percent.[15]

The second form of dynamic income indicator, social mobility, is even more interesting, because it is more innovative from the perspective of measurement. The idea is to measure not an individual's ability to obtain a certain level of income at some point in time, but rather to make his or her way up the income distribution over time. For example, it is now possible to measure the probability that an individual in a given country or locality within a country will move from the category of the poorest 20 percent to the richest 20 percent in a generation. We can then compare social mobility patterns between countries and within countries over time. In the United States, high income inequality has been combined with a reduction in social mobility in recent decades. A 2015 study estimates that "approximately half of parental income advantages are passed on to children" and that "the persistence of advantage is especially large among those raised in the middle to upper reaches of the income distribution," implying that the United States is "very immobile."[16] The US decline in social mobility, now below that of Denmark, is not just an economic problem but a cultural one: social reality, properly measured, collides head-on with the myth of a nation where it is always possible to rise from "rags to riches." Simply put, social mobility indicators contradict the American dream.[17] This also makes static income inequality levels less acceptable. As noted by American economist, advisor to President Eisenhower, and Federal Reserve Bank governor Henry Wallich, "Growth is a substitute for equality of income. As long as there is growth there is hope, and that makes large income differentials tolerable."[18]

To borrow the metaphor of architecture, Americans may have been less concerned so far by the height of the Inequality Building (the gap between the rich and the poor) than by the means to access the higher floors from the lower ones (the "stairs" and "elevator" being higher education and hard work). If these means of ascension are broken or privatized by the wealthiest, then the size of the building might become a problem. This type of indicator points to even greater challenges for public policy, as tax policy might not be enough to contain dynamic inequality; that calls for a dynamic inequality reduction policy. The latter can take the form of education reform for different age groups, with early childhood education and higher education appearing particularly strategic for inequality reduction.

To close this chapter and connect to what follows, we need to ask a final crucial question: What is the effect of income on well-being? Here, we can turn to the Indian philosopher and economist Amartya Sen, who has shown in a long series of influential works the importance of worrying about the capabilities of individuals and groups and not just about income distribution.[19]

Sen is interested in concrete situations of inequality and injustice rather than the conditions of possibility and properties of just institutions. Because of this focus, he is concerned with the real possibilities humans are given in their lives, possibilities that he calls "capabilities." An example he uses frequently to illustrate his line of thought is a person who has a high income but suffers from a serious physical disability and cannot necessarily therefore convert her income into the freedom to lead a life she might deem satisfactory. The capability approach, in other words, is not just concerned with what a person eventually achieves, but cares about the set of substantial freedoms to which the individual actually has access.

Sen provides us with both a theoretical framework to think about freedom and equality at the same time and new instruments to use in order to achieve greater equality and freedom. His reflections have indeed produced a key indicator: the Human Development Index of the United Nations. For Mahbub ul Haq, co-designer with Sen of the first *World Report on Human Development* in 1990,

> The main objective of development is to widen the choices available to people. In principle, these choices can be infinite and can change over time. People often attach value achievements that do not show through at all, or not immediately, in the figures for the income or economic growth: greater access to knowledge, better nutrition and better health services, means more secure existence, some security against crime and physical violence, free time full, political and cultural freedoms and sense of participation in community activities. The objective of development is to create an environment conducive to development so that people can enjoy a long, healthy and creative life.[20]

According to this approach, development goes beyond income and becomes the process of expanding the real freedoms enjoyed by individuals, while poverty is more than just a loss of income: it is truly a deprivation of capabilities.[21] This is why the various human development indicators developed over the years under the auspices of the United Nations consider not only income but other equally important dimensions of individuals' quality of life, such as inequality.

The case of India is particularly interesting in this respect because it highlights the complex relationship among inequality, GDP, and human development. Over the last twenty-five years, India's progress was the eighteenth fastest in the world from the standpoint of the Human Development Index (HDI): life expectancy has increased by ten years and early childhood malnutrition has gone down by seven percentage points (to 39 percent of children under age five). But this progress stalled. The annual rate of the HDI increased by 1.49 percent between 1990 and 2000 and 1.67 percent between 2000 and 2010, but fell to 0.97 percent between 2010 and 2014, all the while India's GDP growth continued on an exponential trajectory, increasing by close to 7 percent a year. The UN points to the fact that inequality alone explains the loss of almost a third of its HDI level, starting with inequality in education, with a little more than 40 percent of Indians reaching the secondary level, in addition to considerable gender inequality.[22]

In the following chapters I explore more precisely how we must go beyond income to expand our understanding of human well-being, starting with the crucial issue of work.

CHAPTER 4

Work

If personal income indicators constitute a clear challenge to GDP and growth as good indicators of human welfare, they do not capture how this income has been acquired and, in particular, do not say anything about that major tenet of economic well-being, work, and its counterpart, leisure.

To see why indicators related to work need to be studied by policy makers, we can first show that the link between growth and employment is more and more dubious. While the relation between the two variables was questioned as early as the 1960s, it is now clear that an increase in GDP growth does not result in an automatic and proportional increase of employment or a reduction of unemployment.

The case of the US economy illustrates this fact. From the 1940s onward, while GDP growth decreased sharply, the link between growth and employment became less and less strong (figure 4.1). At first glance, the overall correlation may seem impressive, but between the 1950s and the 1960s, the same level of growth saw a 10 percent increase in employment. Between the 1970s and the 1980s, the opposite was true. Finally, the increase in growth in the 1990s brought comparatively little job creation compared with the 1980s, while the 20 percent increase in GDP in the 2000s translated into negative net job creation.

This simple graph points to one fundamental indicator of a successful economic strategy: not growth creation, but the intensity of growth in employment, something that will determine the possibility of a reduction in the unemployment rate.

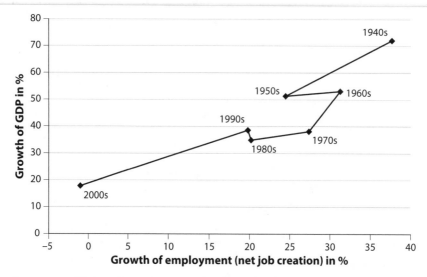

FIGURE 4.1. GDP and employment in the United States, 1940s to 2000s. *Source*: Federal Reserve Economic Data, St. Louis Federal Reserve Bank.

Yet the unemployment rate is fundamentally limited compared to three broader measures of the quality of work in a given economy. It does not take into account the number of people who participate in the labor market. It does not account for how much the workers are being compensated for their effort. Nor does it evaluate their job satisfaction. To begin with, unemployment or underemployment itself is multidimensional. In many countries that produce and publish quality statistics, there is a gap, sometimes quite large, between actual and "official" unemployment. In the United States, the Bureau of Labor Statistics publishes what it euphemistically calls "alternative measures of labor underutilization." One of those metrics measures the "Total unemployed, plus all persons marginally attached to the labor force, plus total employed part-time for economic reasons, as a percent of the civilian labor force plus all persons marginally attached to the labor force."[1] This number reaches close to 10 percent in March 2016, while the official unemployment rate (measuring "Total unemployed, as a percent of the civilian labor force") amounts to 5 percent. In other words, one statistical category is double the size of the other, which completely changes the picture.

Moreover, it is important to distinguish between unemployment rates and employment and participation rates. The US case, again, is enlightening in this respect: while the unemployment rate has now, after hitting the high mark of 10 percent in 2009, regained its pre-crisis level of below 5 percent, the employment rate plummeted by nearly ten points and has increased only slightly since the recovery began, despite all the jobs that have been created. Focusing only on the unemployment rate obscures the loss of work and thus long-term economic dynamism potential that the US economy has suffered with the great recession. Economist Alan B. Krueger has estimated that seven million Americans are excluded from the labor market because of mental and physical suffering, which shows how health can impact employment.[2] An additional indicator should thus be used to qualify the unemployment rate: the labor force participation rate, which has decreased by four percentage points in the United States since the great recession. Even more troubling, lower unemployment can be a sign of people's feeling discouraged and giving up rather than a sign that participation in the labor market is increasing. If fewer people are actively looking for a job, the ratio between those who are searching and those who have been recruited will decline. This was precisely the case at the beginning of 2015 in the United States.

A more fundamental problem is that, while jobs can be created in great numbers, the compensation workers receive for them can simultaneously fall, leading to an illusion of social progress while, in fact, living standards are plummeting, which results in a continuation of the economic crisis by other means rather than a clear exit from it. In Germany, the unemployment rate has fallen sharply since the early 2000s, but pay and conditions have deteriorated in parallel, leading to an increase in poverty, especially among women. In the United States, job creation in the recovery phase did not start before 2015 and is still modest, while the wage levels that preceded the crisis have yet to be regained.

Going further, the quality of jobs according to various other indicators should also be assessed. The International Labor Office adopted the concept of "decent work" to help measure this, writing, "Decent work sums up the aspirations of people in their working lives. It involves opportunities for work that is productive and delivers a fair income, security in the workplace and social protection for families, better prospects for personal development and social integration, freedom for people to express their concerns, organize and participate in the decisions that affect their lives and equality of opportunity and treatment for all women and men."[3] This agenda has been translated into ten broad objectives that can be statistically measured: employment opportunities; adequate earnings and productive work; decent working time (combining work, family, and personal life); work that should be abolished; stability and security of work; equal opportunity and treatment in employment; safe work environment; social security; and social dialogue and employers' and workers' representation. These dimensions are not all equally easy to assess, especially those that fall under the broad category of "well-being at work." Yet, who would deny that job satisfaction is related to productivity and work effort? It is also a strong driver of overall individual well-being and itself depends on many factors, both heterogeneous and subjective. Some of these relate to the obvious characteristics of particular jobs (e.g., working time) but others are more psychological (e.g., job satisfaction).

To see what kind of information such indicators can provide, one can look at the case of the United Kingdom, where in 2016 the unemployment rate was not only one of the lowest in the European Union, but (at close to 5 percent) also one of the lowest it had been for the past ten years. Yet a poll showed the distance between a low unemployment rate and a high level of well-being at work and highlighted some worrying trends that called for policy action.[4] Over half of British workers surveyed (54 percent) felt that their employer did not care about their health and well-being as long as they got their jobs done. Of those who stated their employer did not care about their health and well-being, 48 percent said that this had led to them feeling less motivated, with a third stating they had considered looking for a new job as a result. The poll also showed a connection between well-being at work, health, and productivity. Over a quarter of surveyed employees (29 percent) were unhappy in their jobs, and as overall job satisfaction decreased, the number of sick days taken went up. Respondents who described themselves as happy in their roles were less likely to take sick leave than those who described themselves as unhappy.

Of course, many happy workers can also be found in the UK and beyond, but a hard truth remains: that, while employers and policy

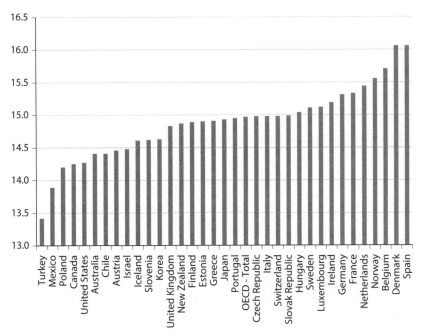

FIGURE 4.2. Non-work time per day, in hours, for OECD countries in 2013.
Source: OECD.

makers want to maximize work, employees most of the time want to
minimize it, that is to say, increase their leisure time. The whole history
of human progress can indeed be read in the light of this negative view
of work: over the ages, the domestication of different energy sources
allowed humans to save on physical effort while technical progress allowed them to reduce the amount of work needed for the production
of goods and services, thus increasing labor productivity. Europeans of
the early twenty-first century spend, on average, only a very small part
of their lives working: less than 10 percent overall (15 percent during
working-age life between the ages of fifteen and sixty-four). In 2013's
approximately 8,700 hours, the annual duration of work on average for
employed people was 1,489 hours in France, 1,669 hours in the UK,
and only 1,388 in Germany.

One of the key issues of modern life is thus to balance work and leisure while maintaining both material well-being and quality of life: in
other words, to be able to optimize the use of time according to one's

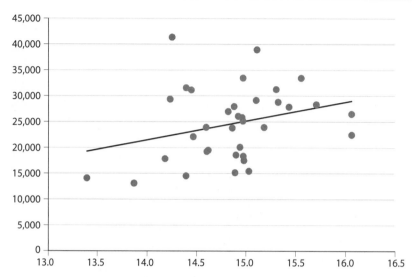

FIGURE 4.3. Leisure and income for OECD countries, 2013. *Source*: OECD. Note: Income is measured as household net adjusted disposable income in US dollars; work-life balance is measured as time devoted to leisure and personal care. This latter indicator measures the minutes (or hours) per day that, on average, full-time employed people spend on leisure and personal-care activities. Leisure includes a wide range of indoor and outdoor activities such as walking and hiking, sports, entertainment and cultural activities, socializing with friends and family, volunteering, taking a nap, playing games, watching television, using computers, and recreational gardening. Personal-care activities include sleeping (but not taking a nap), eating and drinking, and other household or medical or personal services (hygiene, doctor visits, hairdresser, etc.). Travel time related to personal care is also included. The information is generally collected through national Time Use Surveys, in which respondents keep a diary of their activities over representative days for a given period.

preferences.[5] The more people work, the more they might earn income, but the less time they can spend on other activities, such as personal care or leisure. The amount and quality of leisure time is important for people's overall well-being and can bring additional physical and mental health benefits. On average, a full-time worker in the OECD (the group of thirty-five or so most advanced countries on the planet)

TABLE 4.1. How the French spend their days
(activities in hours per day), 1986–2010

	1986	1999	2010
Physiological time	**11:46**	**11:44**	**11:45**
Sleep	8:53	8:43	8:30
Hygiene	0:51	0:48	1:02
Eating	2:02	2:14	2:13
Professional time and training	**3:39**	**3:23**	**3:15**
Work	2:48	2:32	2:27
Commuting	0:20	0:20	0:24
Studies	0:28	0:29	0:24
Domestic time	**3:30**	**3:26**	**3:10**
Cleaning, cooking, laundry, shopping, etc.	2:38	2:30	2:15
Care for children and adults	0:19	0:18	0:23
Housing	0:14	0:18	0:14
Gardening, animal care	0:19	0:20	0:18
Leisure time	**3:27**	**3:55**	**4:04**
Television	1:46	2:07	2:06
Reading	0:27	0:25	0:18
Walks	0:15	0:20	0:17
Games, Internet	0:10	0:16	0:33
Sport	0:08	0:09	0:09
Sociability time (excluding meals)	**0:58**	**0:56**	**0:54**
Conversations, telephone, mail	0:31	0:18	0:19
Tours, receptions	0:20	0:29	0:29
Transport (excluding commuting)	**0:39**	**0:35**	**0:52**
Total	24 h	24 h	24 h

Source: INSEE.

devotes 62 percent of a twenty-four-hour day and night, or close to 15 hours, to personal care (eating, sleeping, etc.) and leisure (socializing with friends and family, hobbies, games, computer and television use, etc.). But there are important variations even among the most developed countries (figure 4.2).

Intuition would lead us to think that income and work are highly related: that the less time one devotes to leisure in order to work, the more income one might expect to earn. Actually, the opposite is true (figure 4.3). This means that some countries are able to invest in leisure or that their workers are productive but have much more leisure time or both.

Other interesting aspects of time use can be explored using leisure data, equality or lack thereof between men and women being one where important progress has been made in recent decades. Studies show that fewer hours in paid work for women do not necessarily result in greater leisure time. Time devoted to leisure is roughly the same for both sexes because of the unaccounted "free labor" that women still largely provide in the household. Some interesting social inertia is also revealed. in France, for example, physiological time (sleeping, eating, hygiene) has remained almost unchanged in the last twenty-five years (table 4.1) while work time has decreased quite a bit. Leisure time has thus increased, but most of this gain has been reinvested by the French in . . . watching television. While the quality of work can be measured, the quality of leisure should also.

CHAPTER 5

Health

Health is probably the most obvious dimension of human well-being, the one that everyone recognizes immediately as the most essential, and it is indeed the first priority of respondents around the world when surveyed about the sources of their personal well-being. It is also the dimension that contrasts most with economic well-being when reduced to the accumulation of money: wealth becomes worthless when illness strikes, the richest life seemingly losing its flavor without the biological or mental faculty to appreciate it. This does not mean that health is not related to economic and pecuniary realities and an economic topic in its own right. Quite the contrary. Economic conditions and social status strongly influence both individuals' and groups' health status and their access to care. Conversely, health status determines many economic capacities, as, for instance, the productivity of workers.

Health can indeed be considered a key human resource because it possesses a direct and indirect dimension: it directly sustains the welfare of individuals here and now, but it also promises well-being tomorrow via the longevity it confers, and it indirectly ensures economic well-being through the ability to work and thus earn a living.

Measuring health means measuring human progress. The most striking stylized fact about the fate of humanity in the twentieth century concerns health: we have seen a greater improvement in human health in the second half of the twentieth century than at any moment in all human history, i.e., the last seven million years. Life expectancy skyrocketed between 1900 and 2000, a century described (and rightly

TABLE 5.1. Average life expectancy at birth, in years, 1000–2000

	1000	1900	2000
Western Europe, Western Offshoots (USA, Canada, Australia), Japan	24	46	78
Latin America, Eastern and Central Europe, Asia (excl. Japan), Africa	24	26	64
World	24	31	66

Source: A. Maddison, *The World Economy: A Millennial Perspective* (Paris: OECD Development Centre, 2001).

so) as eminently violent and destructive. According to historical data gathered by Angus Maddison, during the twentieth century, life expectancy increased, on average, five times more than in the millennium that preceded it (table 5.1).

While this progress is undeniable and lasting (child mortality rates have fallen globally by three-quarters since 1960) it is also unequal. Nations, or more precisely their leaders, can vary as to how much they prioritize health; in other words, they can more or less effectively use more or less of their resources to maintain and increase the health of their citizens. A large gap can thus emerge between the wealth of a country and the health of its inhabitants. One can immediately see the importance of distinguishing between these factors by closely examining the US case.

The Human Development Index (HDI) of the United Nations is of great interest because it addresses the issue of development by aggregating three well-being dimensions: income, health, and education. As opposed to a monolithic vision of development concerned exclusively with the increase in GDP per capita, it gives equal weight to each dimension and can be used to compare the level and evolution of each dimension. According to UN data, in 2011 the United States ranked second behind Norway in terms of income per capita, making it the largest and richest country on the planet. But it is not, according to the same data, the most humanly developed. It ranks only fourth in terms of the aggregate Human Development Index. This is certainly not bad, but merits further clarification. It turns out that the health indicator explains this position: the United States ranks only thirty-third among all nations on the health dimension of the HDI, which means that it is close to the bottom of the list of comparable developed countries.

The significant gap between ranking according to income and according to health (measured by life expectancy at birth) leads us to the problem of the use of resources. The United States, it seems, does not invest enough of its colossal wealth in the health of its inhabitants, or if it does so it is not effective. But is this really the case?

The United Nations uses life expectancy as an outcome indicator for its HDI. One could alternatively use infant mortality or overall morbidity to reflect different facets of the health situation. But there are also other types of indicators, called structural indicators, which specifically provide information about the resources devoted to health. Judging by the level of health expenditure with respect to GDP (in this case a useful indicator to assess the share of economic wealth devoted to health), the United States is actually very far from underinvesting in health. The country is the first in the world, by far, when it comes to health expenditures as a percentage of GDP, which at 18 percent is twice as much as the OECD countries on average, and almost four times the share of health spending in a country such as China. So the mystery only deepens: How is it that the richest country in the world in terms of average income per capita, a country that devotes more of its wealth to health than any other, comes last in the rankings with comparable countries in terms of health outcomes?

To understand this better, we need to use an even better structural indicator. US health care spending is more than 50 percent private, while the average is about 25 percent for the OECD countries. The solution to the American health puzzle then becomes apparent: the ballooning of inefficient private spending leads to a system where the costs are huge compared to its performance.

Understanding this situation, by going beyond GDP and income, makes the need for policy reform clear. The health care reform initiated by Barack Obama in 2009 can be explained by the desire to amend a system in which the human and economic cost had become unbearable. The recent discovery by economists Angus Deaton and Anne Case of very high mortality rates among middle-aged whites in the United States, all the while GDP was growing, is another proof that health status must be studied and measured regardless of a nation's perceived wealth status.[1]

Combining, as we just did, an outcome indicator (life expectancy) and a structural indicator (level of expenditure) is a particularly useful way to understand the improvement in human health, which can be attributed to the significant increase in resources allocated to health since the beginning of the twentieth century. This was manifested by the postwar creation of the welfare state in most developed countries and its financial and institutional expansion since the 1990s by many developing countries, without which medical advances would have remained inaccessible for most people in the world. But the gap remains very large between developed and developing countries, as clearly evidenced by international comparisons of life expectancy. Historical data show that almost an entire stage of life, fifteen years on average, separates the OECD countries from the rest of the world, and there is a difference of forty years, half a lifetime in the developed world, between the countries with the highest and lowest ranking.

But is life expectancy really a good indicator of human health? Life expectancy is the hope that we may have a reasonably long life, but it only captures one aspect of health. Quality of life is at least as important and a long life is not necessarily a good life. This is why this indicator was recently complemented by a new metric: life expectancy in good health.

In technical language, statisticians speak about "disability-free life expectancy"—that is to say, the number of years a person of a given age can expect to live under favorable health conditions. In this perspective, an individual is said to be "healthy" when he or she does not suffer from "functional limitation" or incapacity, this being determined by a questionnaire on a sample of an age group for a given country (for instance, people aged sixty living in the UK). These subjective data are then crossed with objective data on mortality at this age. The process is repeated in this way for all ages and can ultimately determine the number of potential years of healthy life for an individual born in a specific place at a specific time.

One can thus compare countries (i.e., the people living in them) using the two indicators of life expectancy, one more quantitative and objective and the other more qualitative and subjective, to look for any differences. The European statistics agency Eurostat recently introduced such data in the form of the Healthy Life Years (HLY) indicator, which measures the number of remaining years that a man or woman of a certain age is likely to live without disability for all countries of the European Union.[2] Interesting differences appear. France is, for example, the highest country for life expectancy at birth for women, but slips to thirteenth position in terms of healthy life expectancy. This gap highlights important challenges for public policy, in this case the potential flaws in the French health care system for women over a certain age. Comparing trends in HLY and life expectancy thus shows whether extra years of life are healthy years. Another interesting insight is that, while life expectancy continues to progress each year for European countries on average, life expectancy without disability began to stagnate ten years ago. An efficiency plateau seems to have been reached in terms of health policy.

It is important not to overlook the methodological limitations of this indicator of quality of life, particularly the relevance of the questions (the concept of "functional limitation" can be questioned) and biases due to the subjectivity of reporting. This indicator poses the same problem in this respect as self-reported measures of health. (I will come back to the issue of subjectivity in chapters 7 and 8, devoted to happiness and trust.)

Research into other ways to measure the quality of life more objectively has turned to negative valuation indicators. The World Health Organization (WHO) recently produced the disability-adjusted life year, or DALY, which aims to measure "adjusted life years by disability" by adding up the years of life lost due to premature mortality and the years of productive life lost due to disability. Technically, DALYs for a disease or health condition are calculated as the sum of the years of life lost (YLL) due to premature mortality in the population and the years lost due to disability (YLD) for observed cases of the disease or health condition under consideration (where YLL = number of deaths × standard life expectancy at age of death in years, and YLD = number of incident cases × disability weight × average duration of the case until remission or death, in years). According to this method, it can be estimated, for instance, that each year HIV causes the loss of five million DALYs in Zimbabwe and that noncommunicable diseases cause the loss of 731 million DALYs globally.

This indicator provides much better health information than the number of deaths caused by the various calamities that can derail human life. It can also serve to direct medical practices to the most effective interventions. For instance, the British health system has adopted a version of the DALY, the QALY (quality-adjusted life year or year of life adjusted for quality), intended to measure the impact of medical interventions in terms of quality of life. So, for a given medical procedure (e.g., coronary artery bypass surgery), the quantity and the quality of life offered to the patient is measured as a product of number of years of life he or she can expect after the intervention and the quality of life experienced during those years. QALYs thus provide a common currency to assess the extent of the benefits gained from a variety of interventions in terms of health-related quality of life and survival for the patient. But when they are combined with the financial costs of providing the interventions, cost–utility ratios can point to the additional costs required to generate a year of perfect health. This can lead to human life's being given a monetary value if cost–utility ratios are used from the perspective of cost-efficiency (the optimal amount of good health) and not just cost-effectiveness (achieving good health at a low cost).

The best monetary indicators of human life rely on "willingness to pay" to live (or survive), the most widely used being the "value of statistical life" (VSL), which aggregates individuals' willingness to pay for fatal-risk reduction. It represents the economic value to society of reducing the statistical incidence of premature death in the population by one. One method of calculation of VSL relies on aggregating loss of income (and thus consumption) induced by premature death. These indicators are widely used to design regulation policy (on pollution, road accidents, environmental concerns, etc.), but they are highly debatable. First, VSL indicators are, by construction, higher for rich countries than for poorer ones. (The OECD estimates that a life in the United States is worth almost four times more than a life in China.) Second, money not having the same value from one human to the next, it is very difficult to think that the aggregation of heterogeneous preferences yields an accurate result. They can also lead to the wrong policy prescription, advocating implicitly, for instance, for reducing air pollution in rich countries although many more people die of it in developing ones, but at an overall lower economic cost.

As we can see, there are many different types of health indicator, they help give precise information on various aspects of social life, and they also raise a number of important issues, especially ethical ones.

But until now, we have focused on consequentialist and not causal indicators. So, what are the deep determinants of health and how do we measure them?

Here, we find a new class of health indicators: lifestyles and behaviors on the one side, social and environmental conditions on the other, which, combined together, largely determine an individual's health. Lifestyle indicators are concerned with the choices people make, in particular their adoption of risky behaviors. New technologies have fostered innovation in this field and help generate considerable data through individuals monitoring their own health and, more generally, their well-being through the use of connected objects such as smart phones and watches, giving life to the concept of the "quantified self." Yet, contemporary research shows that health is not an individual problem, but rather a collective one, by drawing attention to the growing and often unrecognized social and environmental conditions that determine health, so that health is not merely a biological question but a social issue.

Many studies have highlighted the importance of environmental and social determinants of health, that is to say, the conditions in which people are born, grow up, live, and work. One can observe that, in all countries, regardless of the development level, the richest individuals are healthier than those with fewer resources, which is hardly surprising. Although health has improved dramatically, social inequalities are particularly strong today according to people's place of birth, socio-professional status, level of education, or place of residence. According to WHO, the infant mortality rate (the risk of a baby dying between birth and one year of age) is two per one thousand live births in Iceland and over 120 per one thousand live births in Mozambique. Examples of health inequities also abound within countries: in Bolivia, babies born to women with no education have infant mortality rates greater than one hundred per one thousand live births, while that of babies born to mothers with at least a secondary education is under forty per thousand.

These health inequalities are also dynamic; in other words, they change over time. In the United States in the early 1970s, a sixty-year-old man in the top half of the earnings ladder could expect to live 1.2 years longer than a man of the same age in the bottom half, according to an analysis by the Social Security Administration. By 2001, he could expect to live 5.8 years longer than his poorer counterpart. In a similar vein, the Brookings Institution found that, for men born in 1920, there was a six-year difference in life expectancy between the top 10 percent of earners and the bottom 10 percent. For men born in 1950, that difference had more than doubled to fourteen years.

The World Health Organization has coined the term "health inequities" to designate these gaps and speaks of "avoidable inequalities in health between groups of people within countries and between countries."[3] Clearly, social and economic conditions and their effects on people's lives determine their risk of illness and the actions taken to prevent their becoming ill or treat illness when it occurs. These social determinants of health, which are themselves among the most important health indicators (albeit more as input than outcome indicators), are the circumstances in which people are born, grow up, live, work, and age, and the systems put in place to deal with illness. Major studies in the UK and in the EU have shown how powerful these social determinants of health can be.[4]

Among these social conditions, the environment plays an increasingly important role in determining health. One example of the importance of this "environmental health" and its measure is the impact of a population's exposure to fine particles in developed and emerging countries. The European Environmental Agency has found that air pollution is the single largest environmental health risk in Europe, contributing to serious illnesses such as heart disease, respiratory problems, and cancer, and leading to more than 430,000 premature deaths each year.[5] Studies on the health effects of outdoor air pollution, especially pollution by fine particles, nitrogen dioxide, and ozone, have yielded decisive results. WHO presented at the end of 2013 a comprehensive study classifying air pollution in the category of "carcinogenic certain" and estimated in 2014 that it had led to seven million deaths worldwide in 2012. In China, the observed air pollution has been estimated to contribute to 1.6 million deaths per year, or roughly 17 percent of all deaths in the country.[6]

Indicators of environmental health may seem to be the new frontier of health indicators, but they are nothing new: they go back at least to Hippocrates and his treatise on airs, waters, and places published in the fifth century BCE:

Whoever wishes to investigate medicine properly, should proceed thus: in the first place to consider the seasons of the year, and what effects each of them produces for they are not at all alike, but differ much from themselves in regard to their changes. Then the winds, the hot and the cold, especially such as are common to all countries, and then such as are peculiar to each locality. We must also consider the qualities of the waters, for as they differ from one another in taste and weight, so also do they differ much in their qualities.

In the same manner, when one comes into a city to which he is a stranger, he ought to consider its situation, how it lies as to the winds and the rising of the sun; for its influence is not the same whether it lies to the north or the south, to the rising or to the setting sun. These things one ought to consider most attentively, and concerning the waters which the inhabitants use, whether they be marshy and soft, or hard, and running from elevated and rocky situations, and then if salty and unfit for cooking; and the ground, whether it be naked and deficient in water, or wooded and well watered, and whether it lies in a hollow, confined situation, or is elevated and cold; and the mode in which the inhabitants live, and what are their pursuits, whether they are fond of drinking and eating to excess, and given to indolence, or are fond of exercise and labor, and not given to excess in eating and drinking.[7]

At the global level, evidence shows that environmental risk factors play a role in more than 80 percent of the diseases reported regularly by the World Health Organization. Diseases related to the environment that represent the largest total annual burden in terms of mortality or life years adjusted for disability (DALYs) are diarrhea (sixty-eight million DALYs per year), caused mainly by unsafe water or poor sanitation and hygiene, and lower respiratory tract ailments (thirty-seven million DALYs per year), due mainly to air pollution, including indoor due to defects in the heating system or kitchen. Globally, nearly one-quarter of all deaths and of the total disease burden can be attributed to the environment. The latter rises to nearly one-third in the case of children.

These morbid considerations lead us to a final point, on measuring neither quantity nor quality of life, but death. Here, too, indicators

TABLE 5.2. Causes of death globally, in thousands of people
and % of total deaths, 2013

		% of total
All causes	54,863	
Communicable, maternal, neonatal, and nutritional diseases	11,809	21.50
Noncommunicable diseases	38,267	69.80
Injuries	4,787	8.70
War	31	.06

Source: WHO.

developed in recent years are providing valuable insights on our world. WHO now regularly identifies causes of mortality, measured either in absolute terms by the number of deaths caused or, more finely, as we have seen, by the number of DALYs. What can we see in those data? First, even if overall deaths have increased since 1990 (from forty-seven to fifty-five million annually), the death rate has decreased by almost 25 percent, given the increase in population during this period. More importantly, noncommunicable diseases (NCDs)[8] were responsible for 68 percent (thirty-eight million) of all deaths globally in 2012, up from 60 percent (thirty-one million) in 2000.[9] Communicable, maternal, neonatal, and nutritional conditions collectively were responsible for 23 percent of global deaths, and injuries for 9 percent (table 5.2).

This breakdown sheds light on at least two major contemporary dynamics. The first is that we are living through a global health transition: we are evolving from a time when communicable diseases such as HIV and malaria have predominated to one dominated by noncommunicable or chronic diseases (those that are not passed from person to person and are of long duration and generally slow progression). Between 1990 and 2013, the number of deaths from noncommunicable diseases increased steadily, while deaths from communicable diseases decreased. This transition has major implications for health policy worldwide.

The second lesson is that we are also living through a social transition. War and violence in general now represent a small share of death threats to humans in the world. There are, of course, too many exceptions to this rule, but we live, perhaps as never before in our history, in a peaceful world, which does not contribute for nothing to our well-being. Still, it is necessary that we be able to preserve this relative peace, a goal to which our institutions (to which I devote a later chapter) must be employed.

FOCUS: ARE AMERICANS REALLY RICHER THAN THE FRENCH?

Two Stanford economists recently attempted to measure the difference in standard of living between Europeans and Americans, and more precisely between US and French citizens, by using indicators of well-being rather than standard economic indicators. What they found was most interesting:

GDP per person is markedly lower in France: France had a per capita GDP in 2005 of just 67 percent of the US value. [As a consequence,] consumption per person in France was even lower—only 60 percent of the United States, even adding government consumption to private consumption. . . . [But] life expectancy at birth was around 80 years in France versus 77 years in the United States. Leisure was higher in France: Americans worked 877 hours (per person, not per worker) versus only 535 hours for the French. [Finally, income] inequality was substantially lower in France: the standard deviation of log consumption was around 0.54 in the U.S. but only 0.42 in France. . . .

[In all,] lower mortality, lower inequality, and higher leisure each add roughly 10 percentage points to French welfare in terms of equivalent consumption. Rather than looking like 60 percent of the US value, as it does based solely on consumption, France ends up with consumption-equivalent welfare equal to 92 percent of that in the United States.

Source: Charles I. Jones and Peter J. Klenow, "Beyond GDP? Welfare across Countries and Time." *American Economic Review* 106, no. 9 (2016): 2426–57. http://klenow.com/Jones_Klenow.pdf.

CHAPTER 6

Education

Education is something for which it seems there is an insatiable appetite. This was captured by François Rabelais in his piquant portrait of the giant Gargantua, the story of whose upbringing is one of the first detailed narratives about modern education. Gargantua is raised to become a true Renaissance man whose thirst for knowledge grows endlessly, until "he put himself into such a road and way of studying, that he lost not any one hour in the day, but employed all his time in learning and honest knowledge."[1] The more education, it seems, the better. Yet, the way education is acquired matters as much as the education itself.

To understand this point better, we should start with the idea of education as both the instruction of persons driven by individual motivation and the education of societies driven by the quest for social benefit.

On the first what might be called microdimension, it is clear that education is a key aspect of human well-being beyond its economic utility, although available indicators also show a strong relationship between education levels and social and monetary achievements. All available data point, for instance, to the importance of qualifications for access to employment. The French data on the employment of higher-education graduates are unequivocal: access to employment is always faster for graduates than nongraduates, and the employment rate of graduates is higher than that of nongraduates and increases with the level of education. By the same token, in all OECD countries, unemployment rates decline and employment rates rise with the level of education: on average, the unemployment rate in 2013 was 13.7 percent for adults without a diploma, 8 percent for holders of a diploma of the second degree (i.e., a high-school diploma) or post-baccalaureate professional degree, and 5.3 percent for graduates of higher-education institutions. The respective employment rates of the three categories were, in 2013, 55 percent, 73 percent, and 83 percent.

The benefit to the individual of investing in education can also be assessed by comparing a person's level of compensation with his or her level of qualification. On average across OECD countries in 2013, compared to a level of average earnings normalized to 100 for adults aged 25–64 years, holders of less than a high-school education had a compensation level of 78, those with a high-school degree 108, and those with a higher-education degree 170 (the pay gap being of the same order of magnitude for women and men).

In a similar vein, overall life satisfaction is much higher for graduates than for others: the average value for the whole population in OECD countries in 2012 was 6.2, but reached 7.2 for persons holding a higher-education qualification. This result points to a fundamental truth, which is that education brings with it many other well-being dimensions: income, work, happiness, and also health.

The "human capital" theory, first developed by Gary Becker and Jacob Mincer, posits that individuals self-assess the private benefits and returns of education to determine their investment levels, making education a personal or private investment determined by cost-benefit analysis. But this individualistic way of looking at the goals of education is far too restrictive. Even from a purely economic viewpoint, education brings not just private benefits, but also huge positive externalities to societies. Education is a "merit good," a particular category of goods or services whose external effects are considered so important that the state does not allow the market to freely produce or distribute them. (I will discuss the relevance of the concept of human capital and its definition in chapter 13, devoted to sustainability.)

Indeed, in the philosophical tradition born with Condorcet, public education aims at training not just good professionals but good citizens, to inculcate them with shared values and the basic rules of social life. It also seeks to correct or at least reduce the inequalities resulting from birth and to help students strive for true equality of opportunity. This is the macro dimension of education, a key driver of social well-being and even sustainability beyond individual achievements.

This explains why developed countries so strongly increased their investment in education in the course of the twentieth century. If only 16 percent of people attended secondary school in the United States in 1910, 90 percent were attending by the end of the century. In developing countries, also, huge progress has been made in recent years, with the number of out-of-school children of primary-school age falling from 106 million in 1999 to sixty-eight million in 2008. Even in the poorest countries, average enrollment rates at the primary level have surged above 80 percent.

For developing countries, education matters socially to consolidate demographic transition. Almost universally, women with higher levels of education have fewer children, who live longer. One-half of the 8.2 million fewer deaths of children younger than age five between 1970 and 2009 can be attributed to increased education among women of reproductive age. It is thus fundamental that gender inequality in education has been reduced. Between 1991 and 2007, the ratio of girls to boys in primary and secondary education in the developing world improved from 84 to 96 percent. Education is critical for developed countries as well. Early childhood education is able to reduce inequality and the social problems associated with it; according to economist James Heckman, in the United States, "about 50 percent of the variance in inequality in lifetime earnings is determined by age 18."[2]

The most immediate way to measure this social dimension is to estimate and compare public spending on education. As a share of GDP, this expenditure was between 4 and 6 percent among OECD countries in 2013, from twice to thrice the spending on the military, while a mere century ago this proportion was reversed. This elementary indicator tells us a lot about the evolution of the role of the state in the twentieth century. Data published by the OECD make it possible to refine this assessment by breaking down overall spending on education by levels and per student. In France, in 2011, expenditure per student was a little more than the OECD average, except in primary education; however, it remained far behind countries such as Norway, which devote considerable resources to education at all levels.

The average duration of schooling is also an interesting indicator of social investment in education. Considering this an essential dimension of human development, the UN includes it in the construction of the Human Development Index by making a distinction between current

TABLE 6.1. Current and future levels of education, 2014

	Mean years of schooling	Expected years of schooling
Very high human development	11.8	16.4
High human development	8.2	13.6
Medium human development	6.2	11.8
Low human development	4.5	9.0
World	**7.9**	**12.2**

Source: Human Development Report.

and future education. The education index of the HDI combines mean years of schooling for adults aged 25 years (educational attainment data) and a measure of "potential education" in the form of expected years of schooling for students at all levels of education. The difference between these two indicators is itself an indicator of global education progress to come (table 6.1), while the gap between countries of the world remains quite important in both dimensions.

But how can we measure the quality of education and not just its quantity? Although a little rough and not completely comparable across countries, the simplest indicator of educational outcomes is the proportion of the adult population who hold a higher-education quali-fication. In a comparative study, the OECD estimated that the number of these people in the age group twenty-five to thirty-four years has now reached fifty-one million. Even more important progress can be observed in the first fifteen years of the twenty-first century (figure 6.1): on average, a third of the working-age population has experi-enced tertiary level education, which was reserved for a very small elite group only three or four decades ago.

But the fastest growth in the number of university graduates can be found in emerging economies, a key indicator of social progress beyond economic growth. The distribution of qualified people in the world has been significantly altered in the past decade: in 2000, 17 percent of all higher-education graduates aged twenty-five to thirty-four (ninety-one million) were in the United States, 17 percent in China, and 3 per-cent in France; in 2010, China was home to 18 percent of the world's university graduates (130 million), 14 percent resided in the United States, and again, 3 percent in France. According to OECD projections,

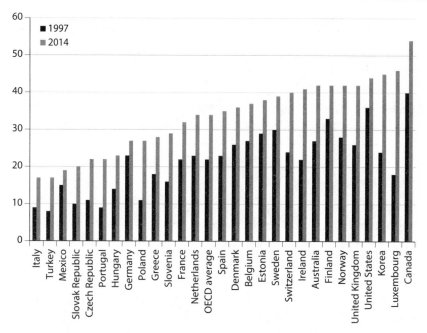

FIGURE 6.1. Tertiary-education attainment among residents aged 25–64 in OECD countries, in %. *Source*: OECD.

by 2020, of a total of over two hundred million university graduates, 29 percent will be in China, 11 percent in the United States, and 2 percent in France. Education levels tell us a lot about the geopolitical evolution of our world.

Yet, the possession of a degree in itself does not say much about the skills effectively mastered. This is the reason why over the last ten years, the Program for International Student Assessment (PISA) has become the most influential education indicator. PISA assesses the extent to which fifteen-year-old students have acquired key knowledge and skills that are essential for full participation in modern societies. According to the OECD, PISA's parent organization, "The assessment focuses on reading, mathematics, science and problem-solving: it purports to assess not only 'what they know, but what they can do with what they know.'"[3] In 2012, for the first time, the first seven PISA spots were occupied by Asian countries or territories. The most recent report (2015) still shows a strong Asian ranking, but Estonia, Finland, and Canada are now in the top ten (table 6.2).

TABLE 6.2. Top twenty countries in PISA scores, 2015

	Science	Reading	Mathematics
Singapore	556	535	564
Japan	538	516	532
Estonia	534	519	520
Chinese Taipei	532	497	542
Finland	531	526	511
Macao (China)	529	509	544
Canada	528	527	516
Vietnam	525	487	495
Hong Kong (China)	523	527	548
Beijing, Shanghai, Jiangsu, Guangdong (China)	518	494	531
South Korea	516	517	524
New Zealand	513	509	495
Slovenia	513	505	510
Australia	510	503	494
United Kingdom	509	498	492
Germany	509	509	506
Netherlands	509	503	512
Switzerland	506	492	521
Northern Ireland	503	521	504
Belgium	502	499	507

Source: OECD/PISA.

Even more interestingly, PISA surveys provide valuable information about inequality in educational performance for each country, an indicator that, even more than the average scores, helps us to understand the functioning of the education system and its effectiveness in achieving a certain equality of opportunity. The case of France is of particular interest with this respect, given the strength of the equality ideal embedded in the Republican school. Simply put, PISA results show that the French school fails in what is supposed to be its core mission: in 2012, in mathematics, close to 12.9 percent of French students had much higher performance than average, but 22.4 percent did not reach the baseline level of scientific literacy, while in

Germany, the corresponding percentages were 17.5 percent and 17.7 percent.

More generally, in France, the influence of social background on students' educational performance is superior to that of other comparable countries. The increase of one unit on the PISA index of economic, social, and cultural background increased math scores an average of thirty-nine points in OECD countries but fifty-seven points in France, the most marked increase in the OECD. (Data for 2015 show that inequality in France has hardly budged.) And things are getting worse, not better: the French education system was more unequal in 2012 than it was nine years before, when a previous PISA assessment was undertaken with social inequality worsening. The OECD notes that "in France if you belong to a disadvantaged background you are clearly less likely to succeed today than in 2003."[4]

Children from immigrant families are at least twice as likely to be among the weakest students. The proportion of students from immigrant families falling below baseline literacy in mathematics does not exceed 16 percent in Australia and Canada, but reached 43 percent in France. This is in sharp contrast with the UK, where students from a first- or second-generation immigrant background perform as well in mathematics as other students. As in the case for income inequality in the United States, education inequality indicators shatter French national mythology and point to the urgent need for powerful policy reforms.

However, the PISA indicators also suggest we should be cautious, even critical, of educational metrics. The performance of South Korean students appeared better in 2012 than that of students in Finland in all areas of knowledge that were tested. (Data from 2015 show Finland a bit ahead of South Korea in reading and science but behind in mathematics.) But is South Korea producing successful, educated students or students educated to succeed on tests? Evidence abounds of the brutality of the South Korean education system: long hours, overwork, the use of corporal punishment, etc. The nation's overall educational performance may be high, but at what cost for the students? By contrast, many studies of Finland's education system show that it teaches students not only to succeed but also to collaborate. What is more, the Finnish system does not rely on constant testing and grading, but on a relationship of trust between students and teachers, who even share the same table at lunchtime.

TABLE 6.3. Percentage of students who agree or strongly agree with the statement "I feel happy at school," top twenty countries, 2012

Indonesia	96
Thailand	94
Peru	94
Albania	94
Colombia	92
Costa Rica	91
Mexico	91
Malaysia	91
Iceland	90
Kazakhstan	90
Israel	89
Uruguay	88
Singapore	88
Chinese Taipei	87
Liechtenstein	87
Norway	87
Croatia	87
Switzerland	87
Spain	87
Portugal	86

Source: OECD/PISA.

It is thus important to qualify the final outcome indicator, the "PISA score," with an indicator pointing to how the performance has been attained. The well-being of students (measured by the percentage who declare themselves happy at school) is a possible candidate: among the twenty PISA top performers in 2012, only four were also in the top twenty for student happiness at school, with South Korea ranking last of all the countries studied (table 6.3).

Several studies on the emotional well-being of US college students report that the United States has declined in recent years, signaling a crisis that educational attainments can hide. The 2013 National College Health Assessment, examining data from 125,000 students from more than 150 colleges and universities, reports that about one-third of US college students had had difficulty functioning in the previous twelve months due to depression, and almost half said they felt over-whelming anxiety during that period, both metrics increasing from the previous wave of assessment.

Student welfare is therefore an important way of measuring the quality of education systems: by acquiring knowledge at the cost of his or her physical or mental health, for example, a student's contribution to society will be affected. The issue of education and that of happiness are therefore intimately related. The difference between a happy and an unhappy education, clearly identified by Rabelais in his *Gargantua*, is the difference between learning to learn and learning to compete. Education policy strictly driven by performance indicators can be so-cially and even individually counterproductive and even destructive.

FOCUS: HUMAN DEVELOPMENT (INCOME, HEALTH, AND EDUCATION) IN RETROSPECT

There is now a rich tradition of "cliometrics," an approach founded by Alfred H. Conrad and John R. Meyer in the 1950s that combines quantitative analysis techniques with historical insights. The cliometric society defines its discipline as the "ap-plication of economic theory and quantitative techniques to de-scribe and explain historical events."[5]

Recently, cliometrics has been applied by Leandro Prados de la Escosura to human development measurement. In order to come up with a synthetic measure of human development, its different dimensions were expressed in index form (the Histori-cal Index of Human Development, or HIHD), with life expec-tancy at birth as a proxy for a healthy life, education measures (literacy, schooling) for access to knowledge, and discounted GDP per head for well-being dimensions other than education and health.

Data thus assembled show that, for all countries of the world, human development grew strongly between 1870 and 2007, its average level jumping from 0.076 to 0.460, or a factor 6 increase. (See first table below.) The first thing to note is that this surge took place while population increased by a factor of 5. But an even more interesting observation is that this human development explosion owes much more to health and education than to GDP

(continued)

(continued)

growth, not only for developed countries but also for developing countries. In fact, improvements in health and education explain 85 percent of the increase in the Human Development Index for the last 140 years, for rich and poor countries alike.

Historical Index of Human Development and Its Components, World, 1870–2007

	HIHD	Life expectancy	Education	Adjusted GDP per capita
1870	0.076	0.038	0.047	0.242
1880	0.083	0.040	0.056	0.255
1890	0.095	0.046	0.069	0.272
1900	0.107	0.054	0.079	0.291
1913	0.122	0.063	0.092	0.318
1929	0.157	0.099	0.117	0.336
1938	0.185	0.119	0.155	0.344
1950	0.210	0.174	0.166	0.323
1960	0.263	0.215	0.224	0.375
1970	0.307	0.263	0.264	0.416
1980	0.334	0.294	0.282	0.450
1990	0.367	0.328	0.308	0.489
2000	0.416	0.372	0.369	0.526
2007	0.460	0.411	0.403	0.589

Annual Average Growth Rate 1870–2007, in %

	HIHD	Contribution of life expectancy	Contribution of education	Contribution of GDP per capita
World	1.3	0.6	0.5	0.2
OECD	1.1	0.5	0.4	0.2
Non-OECD Countries	1.7	0.7	0.8	0.2

Source: Leandro Prados de la Escosura, "World Human Development, 1870–2007," *Review of Income and Wealth* 61, no. 2 (June 2015): 220–47, DOI: 10.1111/roiw.121.

CHAPTER 7

Happiness

Aristotle, in his *Nicomachean Ethics* (written in 350 BCE), makes it clear that happiness is certainly the most elusive dimension of human well-being. In the first chapter of a book intended as a roadmap for his son, he described happiness at once like the most universal aspiration of mankind (what all humans want most dearly, without exception) and the least-shared value (for hardly anyone agrees on its definition). He wrote:

> As far as its name goes, most people virtually agree [about what the good is], since both the many and the cultivated call it happiness, and suppose that living well and doing well are the same as being happy . . . But they disagree about what happiness is, and the many do not give the same answer as the wise.
>
> The many, the most vulgar, would seem to conceive the good and happiness as pleasure . . .
>
> The cultivated people, those active [in politics], conceive the good as honour. . . . This, however, appears to be too superficial to be what we are seeking, since it seems to depend more on those who honour than on the one honoured, whereas we intuitively believe that the good is something of our own and hard to take from us . . .[1]

Happiness, contrary to what French revolutionary Louis de Saint-Just declared in 1794, is not a "new idea in Europe."[2] Greek philosophy more than two thousand years before had devoted much time and attention to it as the horizon of the good life, a line of thought known as *eudaimonia*, which recognized happiness as the sole purpose of human existence. What was really new, during the European and American Enlightenment and, therefore, for our modern world, was the combination of the principle of happiness and of liberty, that is to say, the tolerance for equally worthy but different conceptions of happiness. (Aristotle, for instance, considered the only worthy forms to be higher learning and public life.)

We recognize today that there are almost as many possible forms of happiness as there are humans and that the life of an individual itself contains multiple types of happiness, which constantly evolve. Yesterday's happiness is not necessarily today's. This is particularly true in societies where individualism prevails and leaves the way open for all desires, including those which are commonly held or trivial.

The starting point of any study on happiness must therefore be, as Aristotle rightly pointed out, the recognition of its plurality and multiple meanings. Dictatorial regimes have a clear tendency to define the happiness of their citizens uniformly against their will.

Having accepted the principle of "happiness polyphony," the fact that there can be no substantial definition of happiness blindly applicable to all human beings, can we at least rely on a generic definition? It may be perfectly appropriate to ask whether an individual or a group of people are happy, in their own view, without prejudging the nature of their happiness. It is, then, more than happiness, "the pursuit of happiness" that we can attempt to measure and possibly improve, to borrow the profound words used by Thomas Jefferson in drafting the Declaration of Independence. What should be guaranteed to all citizens by their governments in modern democracies is not happiness, but the pursuit of happiness—that is, the favorable conditions for different forms of happiness to flourish, forms that are up to each person to determine freely. In other words, public authorities should try to guarantee the possibility of a plurality of personal paths to happiness.

Two instruments aimed at measuring the variable nature of happiness have been developed and much improved upon in recent years. The first method is to examine responses of individuals on the emotions they felt during the day or days preceding. These affects can be positive (a romantic encounter, a professional promotion) or negative (a family dispute, bad political news), and the difference between positive and

TABLE 7.1. Happiness in different activities throughout the day

	Happiness (index)	Average hours per day
Sex	4.7	0.2
Socializing after work	4.1	1.1
Dinner	4.0	0.8
Relaxing	3.9	2.2
Lunch	3.9	0.6
Exercising	3.8	0.2
Praying	3.8	0.5
Socializing at work	3.8	1.1
Watching TV	3.6	2.2
Phone at home	3.5	0.9
Napping	3.3	0.9
Cooking	3.2	1.1
Shopping	3.2	0.4
Computer at home	3.1	0.5
Housework	3.0	1.1
Childcare	3.0	1.1
Evening commute	2.8	0.6
Working	2.7	6.9
Morning commute	2.0	0.4

Source: R. Layard. Happiness: Lessons from a New Science (London: Penguin, 2005).

negative affects result in a measure of "net happiness." The second is to count the individuals reporting more positive than negative affects as happy. Their average level of happiness makes it possible to compare different groups within a country or different countries in the world. The limits of these rudimentary instruments are obvious and it may be difficult to make sense of the responses, but the question asked, the experience of negative or positive affects during the day, is highly interesting. For proof, one can look to studies that attempt to measure moments of happiness and misfortune experienced by a particular class of persons, such as US female employees living in the state of Texas. (See table 7.1).

With these simple data (bearing in mind all the limitations attached to them) we can perceive a basic but powerful truth: human life does not seem to be organized according to the principles of happiness. The maximum amount of time is spent on activities that are considered most unpleasant, while the happiest moments of life occupy only five hours in a day. One might wonder why more people do not say more often in surveys that they are unhappy. Given the immediacy of recorded feelings, we can consider that this type of survey really measures pleasure rather than happiness, referring more, to use the Greek philosophy categories, to hedonism than eudaimonism. But another type of happiness reflects a deeper and longer-lasting judgment by individuals on the life they live: the so-called "life satisfaction" or "satisfaction in life." Table 7.2 shows life satisfaction data collected for OECD countries in both 2007 and 2012, the most recent such study.

We can see clearly that, even in comparably rich countries, levels of happiness can differ sharply and that the richest people in terms of their living standards are not necessarily the happiest. We can also observe how social context (in this case the great recession and its aftermath, especially in Greece, Italy, and Spain) can affect life satisfaction. This points to a key question: How does happiness evolve in time and why?

We can start by assessing not the happy or unhappy moments in a day, but what could be called the "life cycle of happiness" or the changes in the level of happiness at different stages of life. These data reveal a philosophical truth about human existence: according to available studies, happiness increases gradually to reach a peak at fifty before decreasing again gradually. In other words, it seems that people learn to be happy.

The Institut national de la statistique et des études économiques (INSEE) recently conducted a survey of this type for French people. They discovered that life satisfaction is relatively high at age twenty, then declines after fifty to grow and peak shortly before seventy, then falling slightly but remaining above the age-twenty level. Patterns of happiness among age groups for all OECD countries (table 7.3) tell a simpler story of a steadily declining happiness with age. Again, the variation in time between 2007 and 2012 is close to negligible, even though the social and economic context has varied greatly, but this is an average.

The US case is even more interesting, with a sharp decline in declared happiness after age twenty-four, followed by a slow increase,

TABLE 7.2. Life satisfaction in OECD countries, 2007 and 2012

	Average points of life satisfaction on an 11-step ladder from 0–10, 2012	Changes in points of life satisfaction between 2007 and 2012
Switzerland	7.8	0.3
Norway	7.7	0.2
Iceland	7.6	0.7
Sweden	7.6	0.4
Denmark	7.5	−0.3
Netherlands	7.5	0.0
Austria	7.4	0.25
Canada	7.4	−0.1
Finland	7.4	−0.3
Australia	7.2	−0.1
New Zealand	7.2	−0.4
Israel	7.1	0.3
Mexico	7.1	0.6
Northern Ireland	7.0	−0.35
Luxembourg	7.0	0.0
United States	7.0	−0.5
Belgium	6.9	−0.3
United Kingdom	6.8	0.0
Germany	6.7	0.3
OECD	**6.6**	**−0.1**
France	6.6	0.0
Chile	6.5	0.8
Czech Republic	6.3	−0.2
Spain	6.3	−0.7
Slovenia	6.1	0.3
Japan	6.0	−0.2
South Korea	6.0	0.2
Poland	5.9	0.0
Slovak Republic	5.9	0.6
Italy	5.8	−0.8
Estonia	5.4	0.1
Turkey	5.3	−0.3
Greece	5.1	−1.5
Portugal	5.0	−0.55
Hungary	4.7	−0.3

Source: OECD.

TABLE 7.3. Happiness by age groups in the OECD (average), 2007 and 2012

	2007	2012
15–24	7.10	7.16
25–34	6.79	6.73
35–49	6.60	6.59
55–64	6.52	6.42
65+	6.40	6.31

Source: OECD.

then a sharp upturn after age sixty-four, so that happiness levels not only return to the levels of ages fifteen through twenty-four but surpass them, forming a U-shaped curve.

One important question raised by these contrasting levels of happiness is what drives them. People may be happy for the same structural reasons or for different ones. It is particularly useful to combine observations of the feeling of happiness with analysis of the potential causes of this feeling. One can thus achieve an overall sense of levels of happiness in order to explore its different facets (love life, health status, professional achievements, income level, etc.). The study of these determinants over the course of a life may help explain the dominance of certain dimensions at particular ages and the way different dimensions might counterbalance each other. It may also help to guide policy toward those issues it can actually influence. So, for instance, while decline in health satisfaction among the elderly is only to be expected, international comparisons reveal significant differences between countries, which the right policies might address. This leads us directly to a central well-known but often misunderstood problem: the relationship between happiness and income.

The empirical studies on this subject, initiated in the first half of the 1970s by Richard Easterlin, rely on the common belief that happiness is a dimension of well-being that is, at least in part, independent of material conditions ("Money does not buy happiness"). But they also reveal sophisticated truths about human aspirations that markets, useful as they are for revealing individual preferences through the consumption of certain goods, cannot tell us: that is, what people experience once they have acquired those goods. In other words, economic transactions can help us understand people's aspirations but not their realization of those aspirations. To relate material conditions to intangible dimensions of well-being, it is important to compare what people do with what they say.

The "Easterlin paradox" sheds light on this issue and consists of three apparently contradictory empirical observations: that, within a society, rich people tend to be much happier than poor people; that, as countries (people) get richer, they do not get happier; and finally, that richer societies tend to be "not that much" happier than poorer ones.

The first observation, that the richest in a given society at a given point of time declare themselves happier than the poor, is confirmed by many studies and is valid both for individuals within a country and between countries at different levels of development. In the United States, reported happiness is concentrated at the highest income levels, while unhappiness is concentrated in the lowest. Among poor families, 22.5 percent are "very dissatisfied" with their lives, against 1.8 percent among the rich, while 23.4 percent of the richest declare themselves "very satisfied" with their lives compared with just 6.7 percent among the poor. This inequality of happiness is confirmed by OECD data showing that, if happiness is measured on a scale of 1 to 7, 4.5 points separate on average the top 10 percent from the bottom 10 percent.

The second finding of the Easterlin paradox is much more puzzling. As income increases over time in a given country, people do not report being happier. The most striking case in recent years is probably that of China, which has seen its per capita income grow exponentially since the early 1990s, while happiness levels have either stagnated or dropped, depending on the survey.[3] Similar data exist for France, the United States, and, more generally, OECD countries. Per capita income has grown very significantly over the past four decades—in most cases, it more than doubled—but happiness levels resemble desperately flat encephalograms. The third and final observation is that an increase in the average income of a country is not accompanied by a proportional improvement in subjective well-being of the population.

Solutions have been offered to this paradox. The most straightforward one is to understand that standard market metrics such as income, wealth, and consumption do not capture all of human well-being. Material wealth is only a part of this, so market metrics should be complemented by nonmonetary indicators of quality of life to fully grasp how happiness occurs and evolves over time. Another solution is to deepen our understanding of the link between income and happiness by enriching economic analysis with greater psychological insights.

The principle of "hedonic adaptation" tells us, in the words of Easterlin, "The utility anticipated ex ante from an increase in consumption turns out ex post to be less than expected, as one adapts to the new level of living, and as the living levels of others improve correspondingly."[4] The principle of "social comparison" teaches us that people's happiness is more strongly affected by the increased income of certain other people with whom they compare themselves than it is by the absolute increase of income for all people.[5]

Whatever the explanation, the Easterlin paradox opens exciting new horizons for research and policy for contemporary societies. The indefinite increase of GDP per capita in any given society will not lead to an increase in human welfare past a certain "point of satiety," when diminishing returns of income on happiness levels are observed. But, given the current nature of economic growth (which, as we know it, is linked to increases in CO_2 emissions), increasing GDP per capita past the point of satiety would be not only useless but counterproductive. Again, the case of China is telling. The Chinese people have lost much of their most vital environmental resources, beginning with drinkable water and breathable air, as a result of hypergrowth, resulting in a gain in terms of happiness that seems negligible or even negative.

The Chinese case raises the question of the determinants of happiness other than income. This most interesting question has been explored using empirical devices that do not just compare reported happiness and income, but evaluate the relative influence of income and other factors such as social relations, level of education, or access to civil liberties and political rights to determine their respective importance in the "happiness equation." A fundamental result then appears: if the relationship between happiness and income appears strong only when these two variables are brought together, it vanishes in part as soon as other determinants such as social relationships and civil liberties are considered. In other words, the simple correlation between GDP per capita and life satisfaction hides other, more important determinants of happiness. If governments want to increase their

TABLE 7.4. Top twenty countries in terms of happiness
(on a scale from 0 to 10), 2014

Switzerland	7.587
Iceland	7.561
Denmark	7.527
Norway	7.522
Canada	7.427
Finland	7.406
Netherlands	7.378
Sweden	7.364
New Zealand	7.286
Australia	7.284
Israel	7.278
Costa Rica	7.226
Austria	7.200
Mexico	7.187
United States	7.119
Brazil	6.983
Luxembourg	6.946
Northern Ireland	6.940
Belgium	6.937
United Arab Emirates	6.901

Source: The World Happiness Report, 2015.

citizens' level of happiness, they should directly improve these drivers. The recent World Happiness Report shows that this fact is true for a large majority of countries, regardless of their level of development. Income is one among many determinants of happiness but it is not the most decisive one: social support is.[6] The top twenty countries of the world in terms of happiness are indeed homogenous regarding not only their high level of happiness, but also the different determinants of this level. (See table 7.4.) On the contrary, the bottom twenty countries vary much more when it comes to the determinants of their respective happiness levels.

This international comparison brings us to a new question: Do the different countries of the world all have the same conception of happiness beyond the universal aspiration to positive social relationships? The tiny country of Bhutan first attempted to empirically define its own path to happiness in 1972, by adopting a holistic rather than an individual-centered policy instrument: the Gross National Happiness index. The fourth Druk Gyalpo, His Majesty Jigme Singye Wangchuck, declaring that "Gross National Happiness" was "more important than Gross National Product," set up a Gross National Happiness Commission with two main issues in mind: (a) The impact of economic development on the environment, and especially on the forest cover of his country; and (b) The impact of economic openness on social cohesion. These issues reflected the cautious and balanced approach to development by Bhutan's monarchy. It also allowed the development of a new metric to assess happiness: "In the GNH Index, unlike certain concepts of happiness in current western literature," said the report, "happiness is itself multidimensional—not measured only by subjective well-being, and not focused narrowly on happiness that begins and ends with oneself and is concerned for and with oneself . . . the pursuit of happiness is collective, though it can be experienced deeply personally."[7] In other words, happiness, according to the Bhutanese, is not only multidimensional but holistic, contrary to the approach centered on more-or-less-immediate life satisfaction. The 2010 version of the Gross National Happiness Index shows how carefully it is built: it defines 758 variables covering all nine domains of GNH (psychological well-being,[8] health, time use, education, cultural diversity and resilience, community vitality, good governance, ecological diversity, and resilience and living standards).

For each indicator, a sufficiency threshold as well as a happiness threshold is applied, which makes it possible to identify two groups: "happy people" (who are extensively and deeply happy) and "not-yet-happy people" (who are unhappy or only just happy). Three major indicators result from this process. The report's abbreviation H stands for "headcount" and represents the percentage of people who do not enjoy sufficiency in six or more domains. In 2010, it was equal to 40.9 percent, meaning that close to 41 percent of Bhutanese people declared themselves "happy" in six or more of the nine domains. A is the average proportion of domains in which people who are not yet happy still lack sufficiency. It shows the breadth of shortfalls: in 2010, it was equal to

TABLE 7.5. Happy and not-so-happy people in Bhutan, 2010 and 2015

	Score range	Percentage of people in 2010 who were . . .	Percentage of people in 2015 who were . . .
Deeply happy	77–100%	8.3	8.4
Extensively happy	66–76%	32.6	35.0
Narrowly happy	50–65%	48.7	47.9
Unhappy	0–49%	10.4	8.8

Source: Gross National Happiness Commission, Royal Government of Bhutan.

43 percent, meaning that the 59 percent of Bhutanese not considered happy lack sufficiency in 43 percent of the domains. The GNH Index is equal to 1 minus the product of two measures. HA (GNH = 1 − HA), so that GNH in 2010 = 1 − (0.59 × 0.434) = 0.743, reflecting both the percentage of Bhutanese who are happy and the percentage of domains in which they are happy. In 2015, compared to 2010, the percentage of extensively or deeply happy people increased from 40.9 percent to 43.4 percent and the GNHI increased by 1.8 percent (table 7.5).[9]

The stated aim of Bhutanese authority is "for all Bhutanese to be extensively or deeply happy." But we can point to several paradoxes of the Bhutanese experience: Bhutan ranks quite low, 141, on the HDI and it is not considered by Freedom House to be a fully free country or a full democracy. (See chapter 8.) Monitoring happiness does not seem to translate into improving important well-being dimensions. What is more, in March 2008, Bhutan ended a century of absolute monarchy by moving toward a constitutional monarchy (parliamentary democracy), but the measured GNH decreased and in 2015, the governance indicator decreased compared to its value in 2010. Finally, the government's concern for the happiness of the Bhutanese people does not extend to the country's Nepali minority, against which widespread and systematic discrimination is well-documented. So does a "happiness policy" make sense?

The theory of "set points" tells us that external circumstances can affect happiness only temporarily and that, once adaptation takes over, people return to their set point so that no happiness policy is really efficient over time. But adaptation can be only partial and shocks can be persistent, as it has been with underemployment since 2008 in many OECD countries. A key question for public authorities is the choice of the right happiness metric, which is difficult but by no means impossible.[10] The best work on happiness leads to fundamental questions about the organization of human life, including the observation that the level of satisfaction is much higher with activities that go beyond interpersonal comparison, such as culture, friendship, or family life (as opposed to professional life). Therefore, a government concerned with the happiness of its citizens can usefully concentrate on finding a better balance between private and professional life. As Easterlin put it, "adaptation and social comparison affect utility more in pecuniary than non-pecuniary domains. The failure of individuals to anticipate that these influences disproportionately undermine utility in the pecuniary domain leads to an excessive allocation of time to pecuniary goals at the expense of non-pecuniary goals, such as family life and health, and reduces well-being. There is need to devise policies that will yield better-informed individual preferences, and thereby increase individual and societal subjective well-being."[11]

The UK has engaged in recent years in an important effort, both on the academic and institutional front, to develop welfare and happiness metrics and translate them into policy. The Office of National Statistics has developed different metrics of life satisfaction, including self-esteem, happiness, and anxiety, which are available for several years and locations.[12]

But we need to be cautious with subjective data, for, as Sen reminds us, "a person who is ill-fed, undernourished, unsheltered, and ill can still be high up in the scale of happiness or desire fulfillment if he or she has learned to have 'realistic' desires and to take pleasures in small mercies." By accepting people's own assessment in such circumstances, "the metric of happiness may, therefore, distort the extent of deprivation in a specific and biased way."[13] The same need for prudence applies to data related to trust.

CHAPTER 8

Trust

As Paul Seabright remarks in *The Company of Strangers: A Natural History of Economic Life*, "the unplanned but sophisticated coordination of modern industrial societies is a remarkable fact that needs an explanation." This explanation, he goes on, "is to be found in the presence of institutions that make human beings willing to treat strangers as honorary friends."[1] In fact, modern ethology teaches us that what makes humans so different from other successful species is not the size of their brains or their individual intelligence, but their collective intelligence through social cooperation (the ability to interact and learn from others outside of the family or clan circle). And trust is the key to social cooperation.

A brief look back at the autumn of 2008, at the height of the financial storm, is enough to convince one that trust is the bedrock of economic activities: without it, no bank, no business, no government can long remain, let alone prosper. Trust reduces the uncertainty inherent in human behavior, turning it into acceptable or unacceptable risk. It also promotes reciprocity and thus accelerates transactions of all kinds. In doing so, it unleashes the power of collective intelligence. For Georg Simmel, one the early experts on trust in sociology, trust was "one of the most important synthetic forces within society" and "without the general trust that people have in each other, society itself would disintegrate."[2] From an economic standpoint, as Kenneth Arrow explained, trust is an "invisible institution." As he described it, "Virtually every commercial transaction has within itself an element of trust, certainly any transaction conducted over a period of time. It can be plausibly argued that much of the economic backwardness in the world can be explained by the lack of mutual confidence."[3]

Starting with political institutions, all social institutions are based on trust, that is to say, on the expectation that human behavior can be relied upon: that the restaurant I dine in meets health and safety standards and that those standards are appropriate, that my bank is not engaged in fraudulent transactions, that the car approaching the pedestrian crossing I am on will stop. Without this set of social beliefs, life quickly becomes impossible, mired in incessant calculations and fear of being let down. As such, trust is just as much an outcome than an input of human welfare: trust indicators give us information on both the reality of well-being and its future possibility. Trust can be desired for itself but also for what it can accomplish in human societies.

So what exactly is trust? It is the belief or hope that human behavior will conform to expectations. Unlike faith, it is a strategic relation between humans—generally two—but sometimes between a person and an institution. It is then mediated by a collective norm and the trust is placed in respect for this norm. It implies an uncertain situation: trust can be betrayed. According to Simmel, "The possession of full knowledge does away with the need of trusting, while complete absence of knowledge makes trust evidently impossible."[4] It supposes a specific goal and given context (that you can't trust everybody all the time on all matters). Finally, it results from personal choice and calculation, which can be founded on something other than reason and influenced by social context.

To measure trust, it is important first to define its different forms. There are essentially three of these: trust in institutions or organizations (which is by far the most important in contemporary societies), trust between people, and finally the problematic notion of "trust in the future," widely used in economic forecasting.

Let's first look at the issue of trust in institutions and observe more closely one of its aspects, confidence in government and its evolution over the last few years. Table 8.1 presents data collected by the OECD on the state of confidence in the government in 2012 and the evolution of this indicator between 2007 and 2012.

These data contain many revealing insights. On the one hand, even if all these OECD countries are considered both democratic and rich (in

TABLE 8.1. Trust in government in OECD countries

	% of positive respondents, 2012	Percentage point change, 2007–2012
Slovak Republic	37	21
Switzerland	77	14
Israel	34	12
United Kingdom	47	11
France	44	8
Poland	27	8
Germany	42	7
Sweden	63	7
Iceland	26	2
New Zealand	61	2
South Korea	23	−1
Italy	28	−2
Norway	66	−2
Turkey	53	−3
Hungary	21	−4
United States	35	−4
OECD	**40**	**−5**
Denmark	53	−6
Japan	17	−7
Luxembourg	74	−8
Mexico	33	−9
Netherlands	57	−9
Czech Republic	17	−10
Australia	42	−11
Chile	32	−11
Austria	38	−12
Canada	52	−12
Spain	34	−14
Estonia	27	−15
Belgium	44	−16
Finland	60	−16
Portugal	23	−22
Slovenia	24	−24
Greece	13	−25
Northern Ireland	35	−28

Source: OECD.

terms of GDP per capita), the differences in the confidence of citizens in their governments are considerable: Norwegians have twice as much trust in their government as do Americans. France is slightly above the average level of confidence in OECD countries. Surprisingly, Japanese citizens have little trust in their government, indicating a social weakness that is impossible to identify with standard economic indicators.

Moreover, confidence in political institutions (here, the government) can exhibit very strong variations over time due to the economic context: Greece lost nearly thirty percentage points with regard to confidence in its government between 2007 and 2012. This is of vital importance because it indicates that Greece has something far more serious than an economic crisis: a civic crisis. (This loss of trust in government is a phenomenon that goes beyond Greece, as the average indicator for the OECD countries lost six points during the same time period.) Greece, which was close to the OECD average in 2007, is now the country where citizens trust the government the least. This is not exactly a surprise, but this development has serious consequences for the country's future.

An interesting connection emerges: the economic context plays an important part in the public's confidence in the government's ability to ensure its well-being (as in the case of Greece) but economic welfare does not guarantee political trust (as in the case of Japan). It is indeed a "civic wealth" that is at least partly independent from material wealth.

We can find further evidence to support this observation by comparing the respective trust that citizens of the United States and Sweden attach to their political institutions. According to data from the World Values Survey, which asks people from different countries about their values, almost 75 percent of Swedes strongly trust their judiciary, compared to only 57 percent of Americans, and 57 percent of Swedes trust their parliament while only 20 percent of Americans trust Congress. This difference is even more striking when one realizes that when respondents were asked about their trust in government in the early 1980s, the subject was more important in the United States than in Sweden. It appears, in light of this indicator, that the United States, which was one of the pioneering nations of representative democracy, has gained significant economic wealth in the last three decades, but at the cost of civic cohesion.

TABLE 8.2. Trust in public institutions in OECD countries
(in % of respondents who say they have trust), 2015

	National government	Judicial system	Education system	Health care system
OECD	40	51	66	71
Maximum	77	85	82	94
Minimum	13	23	44	29

Source: OECD.

These data also highlight a real difference between two countries that, seen from afar, appear to be equally democratic, while in reality their democratic vitality differs greatly. A related issue concerns the respective levels of trust enjoyed by different political institutions. In OECD countries, institutions have a variable level of trust, with trust in the judicial system in almost every country being greater than trust in the government, and institutions instrumental to human development (education and health systems) being considered the most reliable (table 8.2).

The state of institutional confidence tells us about the true state of democracy and alerts us to its potential degradation (as in the US case, where, as measured by the Pew Research Center, the central government receives the support of no more than 20 percent of citizens, a historic low). Political institutions, in other words, can be devitalized by the lack of trust placed in them. This is all the more problematic when institutional trust is supposed to compensate for a lack of interpersonal trust.

This problem of confidence in institutions is indeed fundamental to the development of contemporary societies: trust is both a means to achievement and a result of well-being. As the OECD notes, "A strong social network, or community, can provide emotional support during both good and bad times as well as access to jobs, services, and other material opportunities."[5] Across the OECD, 88 percent of people believe that they know someone they could rely on in time of need.[6] This brings us to the other big dimension of trust: interpersonal trust. Trust between people can be measured through experiments (such as the ultimatum game[7]) or surveys. Unfortunately, the most widely used surveys of interpersonal trust are based on unclear questions, which confuse responses and make it difficult to use them in empirical models.

This is especially true of the so-called "generalized trust" question. This metric contains a grain of truth because it is based on a question, which appears in one form or another in many national and international surveys and actually relates directly to trust. The General Social Survey of the National Opinion Research Center, for instance, asks respondents: "Generally speaking, would you say that most people can be trusted, or that you can't be too careful dealing with people?" The World Values Survey (WVS) asks essentially the same question: "Generally speaking, would you say that most people can be trusted or that you need to be very careful in dealing with people?" But to have any meaning, the concept of trust has to be limited to a specific person (what is called *intuitu personæ* confidence), a group, or an institution in a given context (A trusts B on issue I in the context C). Thus, generalized trust appears as a contradiction in terms: it attempts to measure impersonal trust.

Because this widely used trust indicator is tainted with uncertainty, the results of the (many) studies that use it are necessarily themselves questionable. This is, for instance, the case of the hasty exploitation of generalized trust data that are supposed to show that France is a "society of distrust." The argument relies on the fact that French declare higher levels of interpersonal distrust than others, including citizens of countries suffering civil wars. The key evidence is supposed to be the fact that the WVS's generalized trust indicator ("most people can be trusted") is as low as 20 percent for France. (Germany is at 36 percent and the United States at 38 percent.)

There are many problems with this theory, starting with its internal validity, as data diverge between surveys. (The European Values Survey shows that this indicator is in fact at 26 percent and in France has grown since 1981.) Moreover, as numerous authors emphasize, notably those who have participated in the Russell Sage Foundation's project on trust, the opposite of trust is not distrust or mistrust; it is the absence of trust. And, supposing that generalized trust is a robust concept and the WVS can truly measure it (two controversial conditions), the interpretation corresponding to the observation of a weak rate of positive response to its question is that the society under study

TABLE 8.3. Interpersonal trust in France and Germany, 2006 (in % of respondents)

		France	Germany
Most people can be trusted		18.8	36.8
Trust in people you know personally			
	A lot	67.6	24.1
	A little	27.4	70.1
Trust in people you meet for the first time			
	A lot	6.4	0.8
	A little	38.7	25.3

Source: World Values Survey.

is characterized by an absence of declared trust, or of greater caution. France may thus be a "cautious society" rather than a "society of distrust," which is appreciably different. But, more importantly, the picture of interpersonal trust in France is much more complex than generalized trust, as a simple comparison between France and Germany clearly shows (table 8.3).

We should therefore not confuse different dimensions of trust with one another, especially what political scientist Pascal Perrineau calls "vertical trust" (e.g., trust in institutions) and "horizontal trust" (e.g., trust between people).[8] This distinction allows us to understand that the key to the French political malaise, which is very real, lies in distrust of a number of public institutions, but not all of them. The French have confidence, for instance, in their hospitals, but lack trust in political parties (figure 8.1). The conceptual confusion surrounding the use of generalized trust metrics points to the importance of defining concepts well before attempting to measure them.

Another ill-defined concept in the field of trust is so-called "trust in the future." The question of the evolution of economic agents' confidence over time is certainly of great importance, but it is closer to pessimism and optimism than to trust and confidence. Trust is not the same as faith or hope. To put it simply, the notion of trust in the future is a misnomer, because it is impossible for consumers, producers, or investors to establish a strategic and reciprocal relationship with "the future." This is not to deny that hope or fear for the future play an important role in economic behavior and should be taken into account when making economic forecasts. If consumers say they believe that

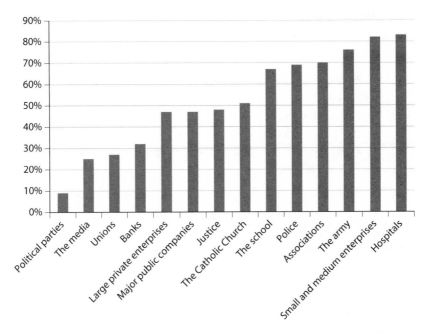

FɪɢᴜʀE 8.1. Trust in institutions in France in 2014, % of respondents. *Source*: Baromètre de la confiance politique du CEVIPOF.

their financial situation will deteriorate in the next six months, it is reasonable to expect that household consumption will slow down and that precautionary savings may accumulate. This subjective indicator of economic well-being often anticipates objective indicators such as inflation or employment; it is valuable information on upcoming trends that can only be obtained by asking individuals about their feelings with regard to the economic situation. This feeling, in turn, informs the authorities about what economic policy they should follow.

In fact, if all the available data collected from individuals and companies point to a decline in private demand (household consumption, business investment) over the next six months, it makes sense to engage without delay in macroeconomic stimulation through lower interest rates or higher public spending, because the policies themselves can take six months to produce an effect. Any government that does not want to be caught improvising must constantly practice the uncertain art of economic forecasting.

One version of this "trust in the future" metric is the Index of Consumer Sentiment of the University of Michigan. To calculate this index, its authors rely on a series of questions asked of US consumers via surveys, among them "We are interested in how people are getting along financially these days. Would you say that you (and your family living there) are better off or worse off financially than you were a year ago?"; "Now looking ahead—do you think that a year from now you (and your family living there) will be better off financially, or worse off, or just about the same as now?"; "Now turning to business conditions in the country as a whole, do you think that during the next twelve months we'll have good times financially, or bad times, or what?"; "Looking ahead, which would you say is more likely—that in the country as a whole we'll have continuous good times during the next five years or so, or that we will have periods of widespread unemployment or depression, or what?"

Using a simple formula, these questions are then translated into an overall score that has been tracked over time since the early 1960s. It is especially interesting to see how the indicator has evolved. In times of economic recessions or downturns, it has provided a warning sign of future economic problems, while in good times, such as the 1990s, it shows how optimism fuels optimism in a positive feedback loop (figure 8.2).

A more sophisticated version of this indicator has been developed over the years by the French statistical agency INSEE. As part of its business survey for households, INSEE calculates and publishes a synthetic indicator called "the confidence of households." The agency asks respondents their feelings about a number of economic trends, both for the country and for themselves personally, and offers them the opportunity to grade their answer: "In your opinion, during the twelve coming months, the standard of living in France, overall . . . will improve significantly/improve a little/remain stationary/deteriorate slightly/significantly degrade"; "Do you think that, over the next twelve months, the financial position of your household will improve significantly/slightly improve/remain stationary/slightly deteriorate/significantly deteriorate?" etc. Results are then aggregated by adding up the positive and negative answers in order to obtain an overall indicator of economic sentiment.

FIGURE 8.2. Index of Consumer Sentiment for the United States, 1961–2016. *Source*: University of Michigan.

Several particularly interesting facts appear when looking at the 2011 data. First, the overall indicator, at 83, was close to its historical low (which is 80) even though the worst of the economic crisis was believed by the majority of French commentators to have occurred two years previously. Second, while GDP grew by close to 1.5 percent in 2011, economic sentiment that same year informed the government that the crisis was far from over in the eyes of a large majority of French people and that future economic times would be difficult. In fact, 2012 saw no economic growth at all in France.

Trust thus appears as an essential dimension of human well-being and its hybrid nature, having both interpersonal and institutional aspects. This allows us to move to the final dimension of human welfare, which is also the key to social well-being: institutions.

CHAPTER 9

Institutions

Institutions are social cooperation in concrete form, the embodiment of the rules and principles that a society chooses to govern itself by and to identify with over time. They are, according to the definition given by economic historian Douglass North, "the humanly devised constraints" that structure political, economic, and social interaction.[1] They can take informal forms (such as taboos, customs, traditions, and codes of conduct of various kinds, such as politeness) or formal ones (such as constitutions, laws, or property rights), and provide the means to enforce these constraints through physical might, education, and persuasion. Governing essentially consists of building, maintaining, and using institutions, preferably good ones.

The need to assess the quality of the institutions that form the bedrock of social cooperation appears obvious. It is necessary even if we adopt a narrowly economic vision of human development; the best available studies on long-run economic development (as measured, for example, by GDP per capita growth) all stress the cardinal importance of institutions as a key condition for increasing the wealth of nations. Institutions, in short, are the rules of the social game, a game played by people and also by organizations such as firms, trade unions, or associations.

Institutions start with the most basic rules and principles that guarantee public order and civil peace, such as domestic law enforcement and justice and defense and diplomacy in the international order, the institutions of the sovereign state. According to a worldview similar to that outlined by Thomas Hobbes in his famous work *Leviathan*, institutions should first seek to establish peace (in the external order) and security (in the internal order).[2]

We do have at our disposal subjective and objective data that can accurately measure how secure the inhabitants of a number of countries feel. Security is certainly one of the most fundamental freedoms, and its loss is painful for human well-being, as we all experience at certain moments (such as during terrorist attacks) or in certain locations (crime hotspots). The OECD rightly notes that "crime may lead to loss of life and property, as well as physical pain, post-traumatic stress, and anxiety. One of the biggest impacts of crime on people's well-being appears to be the feeling of vulnerability that it causes" and provides comparable data on homicide and assault rates.[3] Those data reveal that, while the homicide rate for virtually all OECD countries is under two murders per one hundred thousand inhabitants, the United States stands out among the most developed nations, with a rate of more than five.

But, from the perspective of political liberalism, security is not just about creating a peaceful society; its raison d'être is to support broader civil liberties, which are sometimes grouped together under the term "rule of law" and constitute the foundation of democratic regimes. One can begin to measure the state of political rights and civil liberties in the world using data collected through detailed investigations by Freedom House, an independent organization founded in 1941 in Washington, DC, with the avowed purpose of promoting freedom in a divided world. By using the same methodology throughout the world, Freedom House indicators represent a fundamental value at the heart of the Universal Declaration of Human Rights: the common aspiration of humans to freedom, regardless of where they are born and where they live.

The Freedom House index is formed from two main sets of data dealing with political rights and civil liberties. Political rights are themselves evaluated using a wide set of variables: the subjective perception of the quality of the electoral process, political pluralism, and participation in and functioning of government. Civil liberties are measured by estimating freedom of expression and belief, the rights of associations and organizations (including business and trade unions), respect for the rule of law, and individual rights and personal autonomy (the ability to influence one's own existence). Questions used to assess political rights include "Is the head of government or other main national authority elected through free and fair elections?"; "Are the electoral laws and framework fair?"; and "Is the government free from pervasive corruption?"

By aggregating these two dimensions and assigning a value based on the reported perceptions of citizens, a score on a scale of 1 to 7 is obtained (from most to least free). The numerical scale is then divided into three subcategories: countries considered free, countries that are only partially free, and finally, those that cannot be called free at all.[4]

Looking at the world map of freedom on the Freedom House website, it is immediately apparent that freedom does not simply reflect living standards (GDP per capita) or GDP growth rates in the world. Certainly the richest countries are often the most free, as is the case in Europe or North America, but many exceptions exist beyond the OECD group, such as countries in the Middle East or the "Asian dragons," rich in monetary terms but poor in freedom. Similarly, economic growth does not automatically mean a growth in freedoms. (The case of China, which will be discussed in detail later in this chapter, is emblematic of this discrepancy.) Moreover, interregional and intraregional contrasts are very pronounced: 96 percent of countries are fully free in western Europe, only 45 percent in eastern Europe, 20 percent in sub-Saharan Africa, and only 6 percent in the Middle East and North Africa.

Maybe the most striking reality to emerge from this measurement exercise is the progress of civil liberties over the relatively short period of the last four decades. The Freedom House data go back to the early 1970s. In 1972 there were twice as many nonfree countries as free ones. (See table 9.1.) In 2013, the world had many more free countries (eighty-eight, or 45 percent) than nonfree countries (forty-eight, or 25 percent). Corrected by demographic weighting, these results are a bit less clear-cut: 2.9 billion people live in free countries versus almost 2.5 billion in nonfree countries. The fact remains that more countries and more people are considered free today than at any other time in the long history of humanity. This evolution is very recent and not very well-known, often overshadowed by the economic emergence of what is now called the "global South." Equally important, a new free world has come to life, in which its democratic development is no less spectacular than its economic development.

TABLE 9.1. The march of liberties, 1972–2013

	Free countries		Partially free countries		Nonfree countries	
	Number	%	Number	%	Number	%
2013	88	45	59	30	48	24
2000	86	45	58	30	48	25
1990	65	40	50	30	50	30
1980	51	31	51	31	60	37
1972	44	29	38	25	69	46

Source: Freedom House.

This overall historical progress has been threatened in the last decade: 105 countries have seen a net decline in freedoms, and only sixty-one have experienced a net improvement during that period. The number of countries showing a decline in freedom in 2016 (seventy-two) is the largest since the ten-year slide began. This is why additional metrics, such as freedom of the press or freedom on the Internet, are needed: they can alert to a degradation of civil liberties and political freedoms. Freedoms must be measured in plural ways.[5]

It is also important to measure the dynamic nature of political regimes in a continuous way; this makes it possible to show how elements of political progress and regression can coexist. This is precisely what the Center for Systemic Peace's Polity Project index does, by examining concomitant qualities of democratic and autocratic authority in governing institutions, rather than discrete and mutually exclusive forms of governance. This perspective encompasses a spectrum of governing styles, from fully institutionalized autocracies through mixed, or incoherent, authority regimes (termed "anocracies") to fully institutionalized democracies. The Polity score captures these on a twenty-point scale ranging from −10 (hereditary monarchy) to +10 (consolidated democracy). For the world on average, this score has evolved from 0 in 1950 to −2.5 at the end of the 1970s to +2.5 in the early 2000s and reaches close to 4 today. Here, also, the improvement in the quality of governance in the last five decades is manifest and the story of global economic development is enriched by a narrative of political progress.

Finally, institutional quality must be measured in a functional way in order to evaluate the different components of governance and reveal the possible contradictions between them. This is precisely what the World-wide Governance Indicators (WGI) project data allow us to do. Its framework relies on a simple definition of governance: "the traditions and institutions by which authority in a country is exercised. This includes the process by which governments are selected, monitored, and replaced; the capacity of the government to effectively formulate and implement sound policies; and the respect of citizens and the state for the institutions that govern economic and social interactions among them."[6]

The authors accordingly define and assess six criteria of good governance:

1. Voice and accountability measures the extent to which a country's citizens are able to participate in selecting their government, as well as freedom of expression, freedom of association, and a free media.
2. Political stability and absence of violence measures perceptions of the likelihood that the government will be destabilized or overthrown by unconstitutional or violent means, including terrorism.
3. Government effectiveness measures the quality of public services, the quality of the civil service and the degree of its independence from political pressures, the quality of policy formulation and implementation, and the credibility of the government's commitment to such policies.
4. Regulatory quality measures the ability of the government to formulate and implement sound policies and regulations that permit and promote private sector development.
5. Rule of law assesses the extent to which agents have confidence in and abide by the rules of society, and in particular the quality of contract enforcement, the police, and the courts, as well as the likelihood of crime and violence.
6. Control of corruption estimates the extent to which public power is exercised for private gain, including both petty and grand forms of corruption, as well as "capture" of the state by elites and private interests.[7]

TABLE 9.2. Governance quality in China, 2013

	Governance score (−2.5 to +2.5)	Percentile rank (0 to 100)
Voice and accountability	−1.58	5.21
Political stability and absence of violence	−0.55	27.01
Government effectiveness	−0.03	54.07
Regulatory quality	−0.31	42.58
Rule of law	−0.46	39.81
Control of corruption	−0.35	46.89

Source: Governance Matters.

As in the case of Freedom House, all these data are constructed from surveys of citizens, but also business leaders, officials of the public sector, and the like, and provide a complete and accurate picture of political living conditions. They can help us track the contemporary political evolution of Tunisia, where civil liberties and political rights clearly deteriorated before the revolution: its voice and accountability index fell in absolute terms from −0.45 to −1.37 (roughly three times worse), while it found itself in the bottom 10 percent of the world's countries in 2010 compared to the lowest one-third in 1996. Tunisia is now back to a positive index and ranks in the 55th percentile of the world's countries. The WGI data, more importantly, allow us to perceive how certain political regimes can develop strong and effective but undemocratic governments, as is the case in China (table 9.2).

One can read in these data the subtle political strategy of the current Chinese authorities, a mixture of rigidity and flexibility, openness and control. In terms of the effectiveness of the government and, to a lesser extent, the quality of regulation and control of corruption, China is in a favorable position compared to the rest of the world. But substantial indicators of democracy—respect for the rule of law and, above all, voice and accountability—point to the scale of progress needed on political rights and civil liberties if it wants to be considered as a developed country.

Because they hold the key to effective social cooperation, good institutions are essential to the perpetuation of human communities and societies in time—that is to say, their sustainability, to which I now turn.

FOCUS: QUANTIFYING THE IMPORTANCE
OF (GOOD) INSTITUTIONS

In a unique book, *The Measure of Civilization*, Stanford University historian Ian Morris attempts to quantify the key drivers of what he calls "social development," by which he means "social groups' abilities to master their physical and intellectual environments and get things done in the world." More precisely, he defines social development as "the bundle of technological, subsistence, organizational, and cultural accomplishments through which people feed, clothe, house, and reproduce themselves, explain the world around them, resolve disputes within their communities, extend their power at the expense of other communities, and defend themselves against others' attempts to extend power."[8]

His index has four components: energy capture, social organization, war-making capacity, and information technology. Among those drivers of development, social organization is the closest to institutions as I have tried to define it in chapter 9. It appears that this is actually the key variable accounting for preeminence of either Western or Eastern regions from 1 BCE until the beginning of the Industrial Revolution. The index shows that Western regions were slightly more advanced in 1 BCE, thanks in part to their greater ability to capture energy, but mostly because of better organization (war-making capacity and information technology playing negligible roles). In 600 CE, the East took the lead because of a simultaneous improvement in its organization and a collapse of the organization in Western regions. In 1800, the West took back the lead thanks to an improvement in its organization. It then confirmed it until 1900 with a sharp increase in both organization and energy capture. From 1900 to 2000, the West's organizations improved again (as well as its energy capture), but the factor's impact was dwarfed by the East's war-making capacity and information technology, the latter of which remains the most important factor in the Eastern regions' development.

(continued)

(continued)

East

Energy War-Making Information

	Capture	*Organization*	*Capacity*	*Technology*	*Total*
1 BCE/CE	29.42	4.68	0.08	0.02	34.20
600 CE	29.42	5.63	0.09	0.02	35.16
1800 CE	39.23	10.30	0.12	0.13	49.78
1900 CE	53.40	16.39	1.00	0.30	71.09
2000 CE	113.33	250.00	12.50	189.00	564.83

West

Energy War-Making Information

	Capture	*Organization*	*Capacity*	*Technology*	*Total*
1 BCE/CE	33.78	9.36	0.12	0.04	43.30
600 CE	28.33	1.41	0.04	0.02	29.80
1800 CE	41.41	8.43	0.50	0.29	50.63
1900 CE	100.25	61.80	5.00	3.19	170.24
2000 CE	250.00	156.37	250.00	250.00	906.37

Source: Ian Morris, *Social Development*, 2010, mimeo, http://ianmorris.org /docs/social-development.pdf.

CHAPTER 10

Material Flows

Our habitat, the biosphere, is changing at high speed on a global scale and we—human beings—are responsible. The deep and lasting ecological crises of the twenty-first century (climate change, destruction of biodiversity, degradation of ecosystems) are due to human action, and more specifically to the human domination of terrestrial ecosystems triggered by the first Industrial Revolution. The explosion of human development starting in the late eighteenth century, its acceleration in the 1950s, and its globalization in the 1990s have had two related effects: to bring mankind unprecedented prosperity and to project the biosphere into an unprecedented crisis threatening human well-being.

We can illustrate this dialectic between well-being and sustainability by observing the evolution of the three key metrics of the twentieth century: population, human development, and carbon dioxide (CO_2) emissions (table 10.1).

As the population grew in the first part of the twentieth century, human development improved even faster (contrary to Thomas Malthus's belief), but its ecological impact gradually became unsustainable. CO_2 emissions increased by a factor of 10 between 1900 and 1980, while both population and human development increased by a factor of 3 over the same period. Overall, population and human development both increased by a factor of 4.3, an unprecedented progress, but exactly one-fourth of the CO_2 emissions. These three metrics symbolize the tension of the early twenty-first century between the magnitude of human welfare and its vulnerability, a tension that more than any other determines our world today and justifies that this book

TABLE 10.1. Key metrics for the twentieth century (in factor increase), 1900–2010

	Population	Human development*	CO_2 emissions	GDP
1900	1.0	1.0	1.0	1.0
1930	1.3	1.5	2.0	2.3
1950	1.6	2.0	3.1	2.7
1980	2.9	3.1	10.0	10.2
2000	3.9	3.9	12.7	18.6
2010	4.3	4.3	17.2	26.0

*This historical index of human development combines quantitative measures of income, education, and health.

Source: United Nations, IPCC, Prados de la Escosura.

now turns to the study of sustainability indicators. Notice how GDP blurs the picture by suggesting that human welfare has skyrocketed since 1980, while its overblown value reflects the growing disconnect between human development and economic growth.

Well-being is intimately connected to sustainability: humans thrive on the planet and have greatly improved their condition in the last two centuries because they have learned to make the best of a fundamentally hospitable terrestrial environment. In this context, nothing is more false than to see the biosphere as a dual world formed of two separate entities, man and nature, coexisting but independent of each other. There is, rather, a fundamental interdependence made up of incessant exchanges between the biosphere and the living beings, including humans, that are contained in them.

This chapter intends to clarify the extent of this interdependence and dispel the false belief of an economic world that would turn in a closed circuit. One can do so using the tools of economic analysis but broadening and deepening them. There are, indeed, basically two ways to record inflows and outflows in any given economy. The first is to use the macroeconomic identity, which says that national income is equal to the combination of capital, labor, and other production factors (the "supply"), itself equal to the sum of consumption, investment, foreign trade, and fiscal policy (the "demand"). Economic and monetary flows are recorded here, but these are only second-order streams, surface waters that are constantly fed by the groundwater without which they would dry up, the flow of raw materials and natural resources. We need to make this subterranean infrastructure of the economic system visible.

Material flow analysis, which aims to do this, adds the trade in natural resources to the domestic production and imports and exports of national economic accounts. Direct material flow accounts help to quantify the amount of materials (excluding water and air) that are physically available to economies. The supply (biomass such as wood, metals such as steel, fossil fuels such as oil, other nonmetallic minerals or energy) is made up very simply of domestic extraction and imports, the sum of which forms the raw material of annual intake. Domestic Material Consumption (DMC) represents the total amount of materials used directly by an economy (the annual quantity of raw materials extracted from the domestic territory plus all physical imports minus all physical exports). The metabolic rate of an economy represents the amount of natural resources consumed per capita per year (or DMC per capita).

In other words, the supply of materials, also called the Direct Material Input (DMI), is equal to Domestic Extraction Used (DEU) + Imports (IMP). How materials are used, or demand, is represented by the equation DMI = Direct Material Consumption (DMC) + Exports (EXP).

We should note from the onset of this chapter that there is no fixed relationship between the use of materials and ecological damage. There are differences, for example, between the use of renewable and nonrenewable resources, between sustainable yield management and overharvesting of renewables, and between the use of recycled versus virgin nonrenewables.

We can first try to relate material flows' metrics to demography. For instance, we can calculate that in the European Union (EU) in 2009, the direct input of materials represented 15.5 metric tons per capita per year (12.5 tons divided into materials extracted on European soil and 3 tons of imported materials), allowing material consumption of 14.5 tons and exports of 1 ton. We can immediately see that the EU imports three times more than it exports in terms of natural resources and energy, which means that its prosperity is ensured in part by the rest of the world.

More interestingly, these simple instruments allow us to understand that if the European economy is the world's largest in terms of GDP, it finds itself in a situation of heavy ecological deficit with the rest of the world (in the sense of the flow of natural resources and energy). European countries indeed face strong ecological constraints: they have very little natural resources compared to the rest of the world, high population density, and energy-intensive economies, which is why they have learned to develop resource and energy efficiency. They thus are big importers of commodities such as fossil fuels, minerals, and foodstuffs. One thus needs to think globally in order to assess the environmental impact of Europe and for that, specific metrics are required. These metrics clearly display the geopolitical weakness of the EU, heavily dependent as it is on foreign energy and mining products, which largely explains the region's ecological deficit. They also point to the fact that the ecological cost of Europe's human development is borne in part by the rest of the world.

How can we relate these indicators of material flows to economic activity? One approach is to relate it to the GDP. We then obtain a measure of the material productivity of the economy: how many production units are obtained from a given quantity of natural resources.

We can immediately see the dual benefits of this exercise. First, the concept of productivity is expanded to include natural resources and not just human labor. Second, we can compare countries not only on the basis of their economic wealth, but also on their ability to minimize the use of scarce and valuable natural resources in the production process. The question is not so much which is the richest but which is the most economical. In the EU, the Dutch economy is one of the most efficient, its material productivity reaching more than twice that of its neighbors (figure 10.1). Countries where labor productivity may be very high, such as France, are not necessarily the ones where resource productivity is also the highest.

In general, international comparisons show that the metabolisms (a word used for the human body but that also applies to economies) of the most developed countries are more efficient than those of the least-developed countries, which is not surprising but brings us to an even more interesting question: Is the economy in the long term able

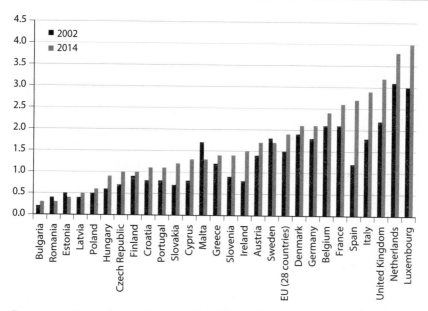

FIGURE 10.1. Resource productivity for EU member states (in euros per kilogram), 2002 and 2014. *Source*: Eurostat.

to use fewer natural resources? Is the economic system becoming more efficient over time?

The answer to this question, which mobilizes the notion of "decoupling" economic activity and consumption of natural resources, is complex. We stick here to two dimensions, which result in two observations widely accepted but disturbing given their contradictory character. The first is that, in the course of the twentieth century, most economies of the world "dematerialized" the economic wealth produced by consuming fewer and fewer natural resources. In other words, productivity (or efficiency) grew. But the second finding is more worrying: that the volume of natural resources consumed by these economies continues to swell. Since the 1950s there has been a considerable increase in the consumption of biomass and metal ores. There has, therefore, been only a relative decoupling between economic activity and the consumption of natural resources. The consumption has grown more slowly than the rate of economic development, but there has been no decline in the quantities consumed over time. In fact, it is quite the

TABLE 10.2. Global materials extraction from 1900–2009

	Total volumes extracted, in 1,000 tons	Metabolic rate: material extraction per capita, in tons per capita per year	Material intensity: material extraction per unit of GDP, in kilograms per 1990 intl. $
1900	7,118,102	4.6	3.6
1910	8,593,573	4.9	3.4
1920	9,624,727	5.0	3.0
1930	11,201,358	5.3	2.9
1940	12,559,916	5.4	2.7
1950	14,149,548	5.6	2.7
1960	19,466,647	6.4	2.3
1970	27,312,490	7.4	2.0
1980	34,818,227	7.8	1.7
1990	41,604,356	7.9	1.5
2000	49,697,913	8.1	1.4
2009	68,140,685	10.0	1.3

Source: F. Krausmann, S. Gingrich, N. Eisenmenger, K H. Erb, H. Haberl, and M. Fischer-Kowalski. "Growth in Global Materials Use, GDP and Population during the 20th Century," *Ecological Economics* 68, no. 10 (2009): 2696–705.

contrary: we have been consuming better and better (i.e., more efficiently) but more and more! The volume of resources extracted has grown by almost a factor of ten, while the metabolic rate, taking into account population growth, has grown by more than a factor of two. Material intensity, taking into account the wealth created, has declined by almost a factor of three (table 10.2).

One indicator allows us to track this evolution precisely: the index of human appropriation of primary resources, a measure of how far humans have gone in "harvesting the biosphere" (to borrow the wonderful phrase by Václav Smil).[1] Between 1910 and 2005, while the human population quadrupled and economic wealth increased seventeenfold, this index doubled. Natural resource consumption has grown less rapidly than population and significantly more slowly than economic wealth. But the fact remains that humans consume twice the volume of resources they did a century ago. This means a global shift in consumption from an average of seven tons of carbon per capita to around fifteen tons, with all the ecological consequences that we know now.

The paradox of decoupling can be further explored by detailing the "Kaya identity" relating carbon emissions to its drivers. Yoichi Kaya calculated in 1990 that energy-related CO_2 emissions = GDP × carbon intensity of growth, or an equivalent, that energy-related CO_2 emissions = GDP × energy intensity of growth × carbon intensity of energy, so that finally energy-related CO_2 emissions = GDP per capita × population × total primary energy supply per unit of GDP × CO_2 emissions per unit of total primary energy supply.[2] The growth rate of CO_2 emissions is thus equivalent to the sum of growth rate of these four components. If we apply this simple breakdown, we can see that the global average growth rate of CO_2 emissions between 1970 and 2004 of 1.9 percent per year is the result of the following annual growth rates: population 1.6 percent + GDP per capita 1.8 percent + energy intensity −1.2 percent + carbon intensity −0.2 percent. In other words, declining carbon and energy intensities have been unable to offset income effects and population growth and, consequently, carbon emissions have risen.

Using the current projections of the Energy Information Agency (table 10.3), we can see that the future is only a little less problematic than the past. Given the growth in population and per capita income in the coming decades (+0.8 percent and +2.8 percent per year, respectively), the decline in energy intensity and carbon intensity (−0.2 percent and −2.1 percent per year, respectively) will lead to only a reduction in the level of the *increase* in emissions instead of a reduction in emissions by volume. Global emissions would, under this likely scenario, increase at 1.3 percent per year in the next three decades, just a little less than their trend the previous three decades (the progress being a decline of just 0.6 percent per year).

While the levels of overall consumption of natural resources and greenhouse gas emissions are indicative of the unsustainable path of human well-being, the indicators we have used so far reflect only part of the human desire for natural resources and suffer from three important limitations. First, they omit a substantial part of the interaction between humans and the biosphere, namely waste. Second, they do not yet count absolutely essential resources for human development

TABLE 10.3. Average annual changes in Kaya factors
by region and country, 2010–2040 (percent per year)

	Carbon intensity of energy supply (CO_2/E)	Energy intensity of economic activity (E/GDP)	Income per person (GDP/POP)	Population (POP)	Carbon dioxide emissions
OECD					
OECD Americas	−0.3	−2.1	1.9	0.8	0.3
United States	−0.3	−2.3	1.8	0.9	0.0
Canada	−0.4	−1.1	1.2	1.0	0.6
Mexico/Chile	−0.4	−1.1	2.9	0.7	2.1
OECD Europe	−0.4	−1.3	1.6	0.3	0.0
OECD Asia	−0.3	−1.0	1.7	−0.1	0.2
Japan	−0.1	−0.6	1.0	−0.4	−0.1
South Korea	−0.5	−1.9	3.2	0.1	0.8
Australia/New Zealand	−0.4	−1.5	1.3	0.9	0.3
Total OECD	**−0.3**	**−1.6**	**1.8**	**0.4**	**0.2**
Non-OECD					
Non-OECD Europe and Eurasia	−0.2	−2.5	3.8	0.0	1.0
Russia	−0.3	−1.7	3.0	−0.2	0.8
Other	−0.2	−2.9	4.3	0.1	1.2
Non-OECD Asia	−0.4	−2.7	4.8	0.6	2.1
China	−0.5	−2.9	5.7	0.0	2.1
India	−0.5	−3.2	5.1	1.0	2.3
Other	−0.2	−2.1	3.3	0.9	1.9
Middle East	−0.2	−0.3	0.7	1.5	1.7
Africa	−0.3	−2.4	2.7	1.8	1.8
Central and South America	−0.3	−1.6	2.5	0.7	1.3
Brazil	−0.3	−1.3	2.9	0.5	1.8
Other	−0.1	−2.0	2.3	0.9	1.0
Total non-OECD	**−0.3**	**−2.5**	**3.8**	**0.9**	**1.9**
Total world	**−0.2**	**−2.1**	**2.8**	**0.8**	**1.3**

Source: International Energy Outlook 2013, EIA.

TABLE 10.4. The cost of food in water (global average), 2008

1 beer (250 ml)	75 liters
1 kg potatoes	250 liters
1 kg apples	700 liters
1 kg chicken	3,900 liters
1 kg beef	15,500 liters
1 kg chocolate	24,000 liters

Source: A. Y. Hoekstra and A. K. Chapagain. *Globalization of Water: Sharing the Planet's Freshwater Resources* (Oxford, UK: Blackwell/ Water Footprint Network, 2008).

such as water. And third, they still rely on GDP as the reference metric from which a decoupling of environmental damage and natural resource consumption is sought; genuine decoupling should associate human development and not economic growth with reduced material consumption.[3]

How much attention is paid to the creation of waste throughout the production process relates to the two increasingly conflicting visions of the economic system. The first, the "linear economy," adopts a production that involves excessive extracting of natural resources (e.g., mining), excessive energy consumption, mainly of fossil fuels (e.g., coal), and a large release of nonbiodegradable waste (e.g., plastic) at the end of the consumption process. The alternative approach is termed "circular." It limits the demands made on the biosphere, fosters the use of renewable energy, and reduces waste by using recyclable materials. Today many waste indicators exist and circular economy indicators are being developed.

Water consumption also needs to enter material flow analysis. We can, of course, measure domestic water consumption (which is excessive in many Southern European countries, which are in a chronic state of water stress) or water imports. But it is also important to measure the flow of "virtual water," water that is incorporated into agricultural products or manufactured goods and is an ecological cost imposed on the producer country. Indeed, virtual water is used in great quantities to produce many manufactured goods (table 10.4), the content of a commodity, good, or service being the volume of fresh water used to produce the product, measured at the place where the product was actually produced (production-site definition).

All European countries import and export water in virtual form and each leaves a distinct water "footprint."[4] But in the end, all countries in Europe have a net import.

This last consideration encourages us to think further about the question of hidden flows of consumed materials and reconsider the possibility of decoupling, or disconnecting the increase in human well-being from the consumption of natural resources and the environmental damage it causes in the biosphere. The goal of these indicators for public policy is not small: in the coming decades these instruments will allow us to develop sustainable economic systems.

The challenge posed to developed countries is that, yes, they are often more advanced in terms of good environmental practices on their own soil, but in so doing they are only paying attention to part of their environmental footprint, one that is visible and directly under their control. As their level of economic development increases, countries reduce the levels of natural resource extraction in their own territory but do not reduce their consumption of natural resources. Instead they outsource the environmental damage caused by their economic development to countries that are willing to pay the environmental costs in exchange for pay. But this cost is often paid by the poorest people who see little of the actual money. To measure this phenomenon, a real indicator of the overall impact of economic development of a country is needed. Such a metric exists, and has been called the "material footprint."

It turns out that, for the countries studied, material trade is three times larger in volume (tons) than economic trade. It also turns out that, where natural resource consumption is properly measured, even relative decoupling appears to be an illusion: for 10 percent of GDP growth, the material footprint increases by 6 percent. As the authors of a 2015 study note, "Our findings call into question the sole use of current resource productivity indicators in policy making and suggest the necessity of an additional focus on consumption based accounting for natural resource use."[5]

Indicators such as material productivity are therefore not an accurate enough guide to the ecological virtue of nations. Some European countries are exemplary in their use of natural resources, but they fail to include those that have been imported as manufactured or agricultural products. (It takes about one hundred kilograms of CO_2 to make a computer tablet and about fifty liters of water to produce an orange.) When these hidden flows are added, the European Union's material footprint is growing as fast as GDP or faster. The case of France is typical: if the apparent domestic consumption of material per capita in 2010 was twelve tons, real consumption of materials (taking into account hidden flows) was fifteen. This is also true for emissions of greenhouse gases, which were only the equivalent of 7.7 tons of CO_2 per capita in 2010, but 11.6, a third more, when carbon embedded in consumer products was also recorded. According to these calculations, CO_2 emissions have not declined by 10 percent since 1990 as UN data show, but increased by 11 percent over this period.

Other equivalent metrics have been developed recently, such as total material requirement (TMR), which measures the material basis of an economy. It includes all direct material inputs (DMI) into the economy, unused domestic flows (UDE), and the indirect flows associated with imports. Total material consumption (TMC) quantifies the amounts of materials used, both directly and indirectly, for domestic production and consumption activities. In short, TMC is equal to TMR less exports and their indirect flows.

This indicator shows that, on average, the amount of natural resources consumed in the richest countries doubles when all the flows are accounted for, so that the illusion of decoupling within national borders is again unveiled. It also shows wide differences in metabolic rates when they are counted through TMC per capita: the most developed countries in Europe consume almost half as much as the OECD countries in the Americas (table 10.5).

What is more, recent data from the UN using this methodology show that the increased consumption of natural resources is unequally distributed among the world's countries. If global material use has tripled over the past four decades, with annual global extraction growing from twenty-two billion tons in 1970 to seventy billion tons in 2010, the annual per capita material footprint for the Asia-Pacific region, Latin America and the Caribbean, and West Asia is between nine and ten tons, or half that of Europe and North America, which average about

TABLE 10.5. Comparing DMC and TMC, in tons per capita, 2014

	Domestic material consumption per capita	Total material consumption per capita
OECD	17	34
OECD America	21	40
OECD Europe	14	27

Source: OECD.

twenty to twenty-five tons per person. By contrast, Africa has an average material footprint of below three tons per capita.

It is thus clear that we need to link the analysis of human development to natural resource consumption and environmental damage, and make progress toward understanding and measuring the concept of sustainability building on that connection. A crucial part of this effort is to gauge as precisely as we can the amount of damage socially differentiated human societies have done to the biosphere and the socially differentiated impact these degradations entail.

CHAPTER 11

State of the Biosphere

How can we measure the global environmental change set in motion by the industrial revolutions and the subsequent explosion of human well-being in the new era now referred to as the Anthropocene?[1] We can first try to represent the processes at work (figure 11.1). Growing economic activity and current consumption and production patterns have given rise to three major ecological disruptions—of land and soil, global biochemistry, and life on Earth—which eventually led to the three great contemporary ecological crises: climate change, destruction of biodiversity, and ecosystems degradation.

Humans, who made their appearance only seven million years ago, have, in two short centuries, completely taken possession of a planet 4.5 billion years old and imposed on virtually all forms of life, including those which first appeared 3.5 billion years ago, the consequences of the explosion in their well-being. A vast amount of data have been gathered to assess what is now referred to as the "great acceleration."[2] But how can we precisely measure the three ecological crises that, in the end, hold the key to our well-being?[3] Let's start with biodiversity, which is the support system of our well-being. The main types of indicators are those that relate to the state of biodiversity and those that relate to the destruction of biodiversity by humans.

Biodiversity (biological diversity) defines the variety of all living things resulting from the process of evolution described by Charles Darwin and Alfred Russel Wallace in the nineteenth century. It is typically considered at three levels: species diversity, genetic diversity, and ecosystem diversity.

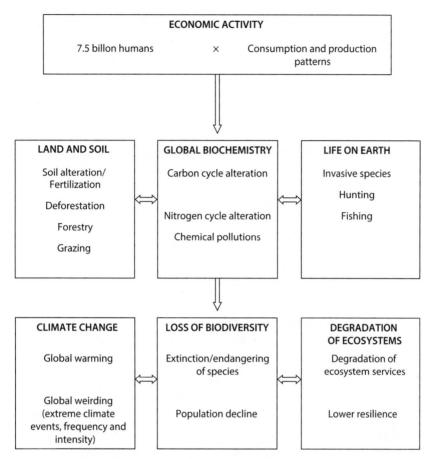

FIGURE 11.1. The anthropogenic transformation of the planet. *Source*: Adapted from Peter M. Vitousek, Harold A. Mooney, Jane Lubchenco, and Jerry M. Melillo, "Human Domination of Earth's Ecosystems," *Science* 277, no. 5325 (July 25, 1997): 494–99.

Close to 2.4 million species have been identified and named. (A 2014 estimate counted 1.9 million animals and four hundred thousand plants.) But estimates of the total number of species on Earth could be ten times greater, because we are only aware of a small fraction of them. For instance, we know very little about the species that live in the deep oceans, which represent 95 percent of the biosphere and 70 percent of our planet's surface. We also know very little about microbial species, seven hundred distinct varieties of which have been identified in the human mouth alone.

There is now a widespread scientific consensus that the biosphere is on the verge of a "sixth extinction," a massive destruction of life a thousand times quicker than would happen naturally and caused mostly by the destruction of animal and plant habitats by humans. There are two ways to measure this crisis with two different indicators. The first one is static and gives a snapshot of the numbers of species threatened among those monitored. The International Union for Conservation of Nature publishes the "Red List" of such species and estimates this proportion at around 30 percent; in 2015, among the 79,837 species monitored, a total of 23,250 were considered under threat.

The World Wildlife Fund has, on the other end, built a dynamic metric, the Living Planet Index (LPI), which is a measure of the state of the world's biological diversity based on population trends of vertebrate species from terrestrial, freshwater, and marine habitats. The LPI has been adopted by the Convention of Biological Diversity (CBD) with the explicit objective of making progress in the preservation of biodiversity. Since 1970, a 30 to 50 percent decline in biodiversity has been observed.[4] (A change in methodology in 2014 gave more weight to areas in which biodiversity loss is more pronounced.)

Biodiversity is essential to human well-being, sustaining ecosystem services that support our economies and societies. This is why the destruction of biodiversity is closely linked to the degradation of ecosystems, the second ecological crisis that needs careful monitoring and empirical assessment.

According to Eugene P. Odum, an ecosystem is a "natural unit that includes living and nonliving parts interacting to produce a stable system in which the exchange of materials between the living and nonliving parts follows circular paths."[5] In contrast to ecosystem functions, ecosystem services are, simply put, the many benefits people obtain from ecosystems. Their very name implies access and demand by humans. Ecosystems indeed freely provide goods and services that translate into benefits, among them nutrition, access to clean air and water, health, safety, and enjoyment, which in turn increase human well-being. The British government describes these as "the benefits provided by ecosystems that contribute to making human life both possible and worth living."[6]

The Millennium Ecosystem Assessment (MA), called for by United Nations Secretary-General Kofi Annan in 2000 and initiated in 2001, assessed the consequences of ecosystem change for human well-being.[7] The MA organized ecosystem services into four categories: provisioning services, regulating services, cultural services, and supporting services. Its conclusion was that 60 percent of ecosystem services were degraded or on the verge of degradation (eighteen services out of twenty-four). The Economics of Ecosystems and Biodiversity (TEEB), a project started in 2007, proposed a typology of twenty-two ecosystem services divided into four main categories, mainly following the MA classification (supporting services such as habitat for species, provisioning services such as providing food or fresh water, regulating services such as regulation of local climate and air quality, and cultural services such as recreation and mental and physical health).

There have been several attempts to evaluate the economic value of ecosystem services. A 1997 study proposed a comparison between well-being flows derived from manufactured capital, using GDP as a proxy, and those derived from natural capital.[8] (See chapter 13 for a discussion of these concepts.) Well-being derived from natural capital was estimated to be worth 1.8 times more than well-being derived from manufactured capital. In 2014, an update of this study was published, but conveyed confusing messages about the state of ecosystem services.[9] The first message was that ecosystem services had improved (because of improvement in methodology and data, i.e., human intelligence); the second was that they have declined because of human carelessness. More precisely, the economic value of nearly all ecosystem services had increased because, according to the authors, the TEEB dataset provided more accurate values of ecosystem services, which were higher than their 1997 estimates for all but two ecosystem services, estuaries and swamps. But, since 1997, the volume/area of ecosystems had simultaneously decreased because of negative change in coral reefs, forest cover, wetlands, and tundra. Overall, this study estimates the increase in value to be twenty-three times greater than the decrease in volume.[10] Apart from the many methodological problems raised by these studies, their interest for policy appears very limited.

Much more interesting is the economic evaluation of local ecosystem services in order to improve the management of natural resources.

The 2009–2011 UK National Ecosystem Assessment was undertaken precisely to "further the understanding of the economic and social value of nature" and "support the inclusion of natural capital in the UK's National Accounts."[11] One aspect of this work is thus explicitly to change policy. The case study of forests is of particular interest in this regard. Conventional cost-benefit analysis shows that, under the market value policy option, an implementation cost of £79 million per year (in terms of planting and landowner compensation) results in an annual net loss to society of £65 million. When the planting strategy takes into account greenhouse gas emissions and recreational values, the annual implementation costs increase to £231 million. But under this social value policy option, society actually enjoys a net gain of £546 million per year. Another example of local ecosystem services valuation is the Natural Capital Project at Stanford University.[12]

Finally, we turn to the most talked-about ecological crisis, climate change, which is really a crisis of one particular ecosystem service, climate regulation. Here, also, it is important to show the connection between human systems and natural systems and insist not just on climate-change indicators but also on climate justice metrics.

Three core indicators of climate change are by now well-known. Annual global emissions from fossil fuel and industry represent around thirty-six gigatons of CO_2, an increase of 60 percent since 1990; their concentration is now at more than 400 ppm; and temperatures compared with preindustrial levels have already risen by 1°C and will possibly reach 3 to 6 degrees by the end of the twenty-first century. These are physical limits, but also ethical and political boundaries, since their value depends on collective deliberation and action and public policy.

The concept of a carbon budget, included in the 2014 Intergovernmental Panel on Climate Change (IPCC) report, establishes that the countries of the world can emit a finite amount of greenhouse gas emissions in the three to four coming decades in order to remain within acceptable limits of global warming.[13] The IPCC has adopted a carbon budget of one thousand billion long-scale tons. Estimates, of course, vary depending on the assumptions and objectives. If we accept the calculations of the Global Carbon Project, which inspired the IPCC report, the cumulative volume of CO_2 emissions since 1870 should not exceed a total of 3,200 gigatons in 2040 in order to retain a 66 percent chance of maintaining global temperature below two degrees of warming by the end of the century compared to preindustrial times. In 2014, about two thousand gigatons of this budget had already been consumed/produced. (Past cumulative emissions amounted to approximately 1,330 tons, while "committed" emissions, those that cannot be avoided given existing infrastructures, were about 730 tons.) Knowing that the current rate of emission is about thirty-seven gigatons a year, at this rate, the 1,200 remaining gigatons would be consumed in about thirty years. But by whom?

This carbon budget is the result of the physical limits of the biosphere, whose forests, seas, and oceans can currently absorb around 55 percent of emissions of anthropogenic greenhouse effect, the remaining 45 percent aggravating the greenhouse effect.[14] But two critical dimensions of this physical limit refer to political and social choices. Issues of intergenerational and intragenerational justice are central to both the choice of global warming limit that is set and the criteria by which the allocation of the carbon budget is made.

First, the safety threshold of two degrees of global warming is not unanimously accepted. Some countries, including the Pacific island states, consider that crossing the limit of 1.5 degrees puts them in serious danger. This is a direct result of differences in the adaptive capacity of countries according to their exposure and sensitivity to climate change. Choosing 1.5 rather than two degrees as a limit not to cross at the end of the twenty-first century (given that the limit of one degree of warming was passed in 2015) implies a lower overall carbon budget. The Paris Agreement, signed after the United Nations Climate Change Conference in December 2015 (COP 21) and entered into force in 2016 opts for a middle ground, a warming of between 1.5 and two degrees precisely to acknowledge claims from the most vulnerable states. But current emissions trajectories would lead to a degree of warming that could reach twice that level.

Once the carbon budget is determined, the criteria adopted for its allocation—the real indicators of climate justice—arise. This issue is still undecided, as the negotiations in Paris made no progress on this front. The study the Global Carbon Project published at the end of 2014 is a proposal for an equitable distribution of the climate burden on the basis of two criteria considered on an equal footing: the current share of each country in global emissions and their share in the world population.[15] It is actually possible to design a more comprehensive but relatively simple system of distribution based on four criteria of climate justice: demography, economic development, spatial responsibility, and temporal responsibility. Many other options have been put forward in recent years, such as the insightful "responsibility and capacity" indicator designed by the Greenhouse Development Rights Framework proposed by Paul Baer, Tom Athanasiou, and Sivan Kartha in 2008.[16]

The demographic criterion is that of per capita emissions. China may be by far the largest emitter of CO_2 in the world, but it is also the most populous country on the planet. The space criterion takes into account not emissions from production. but emissions from consumption. Economic development is slightly more complex because it can give rise to various interpretations, but we can acknowledge an equivalent right to development for all countries of the globe, so that the carbon budget is really a development budget and the deviation from a reference level (e.g., the Human Development Index) entitles a country to more CO_2 emissions for the future. A final criterion pays tribute to the "historical responsibility" of rich countries for climate change.[17] The combination of these leads to interesting results, chief among them a halving of the carbon budget because of the enhanced efforts required by some countries when justice principles are applied instead of an equal right to consume (table 11.1).

There is still one important climate variable to consider. If the contents of the thirty-two-page Paris Agreement and its related decisions had to be summarized in a single phrase, we could say that ambitions have never been so high but constraints so low. This is the basic trade-off in the text, and was undoubtedly the condition for its adoption by all the world's countries. The expectation had been that COP 21 would extend to the emerging markets, starting with China and India, the binding commitments agreed in Kyoto eighteen years before by the developed countries. What took place was exactly the opposite. Under the leadership of the US government, which dominated this round of negotiations from start to finish, and where the EU was sorely absent, every member nation in Annex I of the Kyoto Protocol was effectively released from any legal constraints on the nature of its commitments in the fight against climate change. The latter now amount to voluntary

TABLE 11.1. A simple model of climate justice

Top 20 CO$_2$ emitters: 76% of global emissions	% of the global average of consumption emissions per capita, averaged over 1990–2012	% of the global average of HDI, averaged over 1990–2012	Average of distance to 100 of (1) and (2) (in %)	Equal distribution* of 75% of 1200bn tons of CO$_2$ (in bn tons)*	Carbon budget per country: = (4) + or − (3) (in bn tons)
	(1)	(2)	(3)	(4)	
India	27	75	49	45	67
Indonesia	30	95	38	45	62
Brazil	43	106	26	45	56
Thailand	70	102	14	45	51
China	85	97	9	45	49
Mexico	83	108	5	45	47
Turkey	96	104	0	45	45
Iran	123	103	−13	45	39
South Africa	137	94	−15	45	38
France	187	122	−55	45	20
Italy	210	121	−65	45	16
UK	232	123	−78	45	10
South Korea	233	121	−77	45	10
Russia	253	112	−82	45	8
Japan	249	123	−86	45	6
Germany	280	124	−102	45	−1
Saudi Arabia	296	114	−105	45	−2
Australia	319	127	−123	45	−10
Canada	361	125	−143	45	−19
United States	391	125	−158	45	−26
Total				900	466

*An alternative would be to allocate this universal endowment to countries based on their respective populations, but this would mean taking population into account twice.

Source: Author. Data from Global Carbon Project and UN.

contributions that countries determine on their own and without reference to a common goal.

In doing this, the Paris Agreement gave rise to a new climate indicator, which we can accurately track over the coming years: the factor of climate inconsistency, which compares objectives and means. At the end of COP 21, this ratio was in the range of 1.35 to 2. (The climate objective chosen, specified in Article 2, lies between 1.5 and 2 degrees Celsius, whereas the sum of national voluntary contributions pledged to reach this would lead to warming of 2.7 to 3 degrees.) In a more positive version, the factor of climate lucidity lies between 50 and 74 percent. The question facing us now is thus the following: how to deal with climate inconsistency by bringing the means deployed into line with the ambitions declared, bringing the climate inconsistency factor to 1 or the climate lucidity factor to 100 percent.

In closing this chapter, a reference is needed to a recent influential framework that attempts to take the full measure of our ecological crises: the so-called "planetary boundaries" approach. In the most recent version, dated 2015, nine biosphere processes are taken into account and evaluated, among them climate change, stratospheric ozone depletion, nitrogen or phosphorus inputs to the biosphere, ocean acidification, and soil use. The authors conclude that "Four of nine planetary boundaries have now been crossed as a result of human activity: climate change, loss of biosphere integrity, land-system change, [and] altered biogeochemical cycles (phosphorus and nitrogen)."[18] This study is symbolic of currently prevalent models of ecological crises, which have in common a relative lack of attention to the social dimension. Environmental risk is certainly a collective and global horizon, but it is socially differentiated.

The Anthropocene narrative presents us with a human species that, on account of its overweening collective intelligence, has set in motion a geological revolution, to the perverse effects of which the human species as a whole now finds itself subject. The planetary boundaries approach puts forward, along similar lines, the notion of global thresholds beyond which the environment would no longer be safe for human beings, without social distinction. Both representations, which undoubtedly have their uses, have the same shortcoming and point up the same need, namely, for an ecological analysis that is *socially differentiated.* Who is responsible for what with what consequences for whom? Such is the twofold *social-ecological* question that brings the change in natural systems into interplay with the dynamic of social systems.

The essential point requiring emphasis here is that human beings, in the face of environmental crisis, are equal neither in terms of responsibility nor vulnerability. We thus need social-ecological indicators linking issues of sustainability with issues of justice, a topic we will explore further in the coming chapters on sustainability analysis.

CHAPTER 12

Environmental Performance

China has grown at an impressive rate so far this century, doubling its GDP between 2000 and 2015, but how should we evaluate its real development, taking into account the mounting ecological problems that the country faces, starting with water and air pollution? Different metrics have been developed to assess environmental performance or the way a country is able to manage its natural resources, but this should not be confused with sustainability analysis and measurement, which implies a dynamic approach.

The most influential environmental performance indicator is the ecological footprint, which tracks the area of biologically productive land and water required to provide the renewable resources people use, and includes the space needed for infrastructure and vegetation to absorb waste carbon dioxide (CO_2).[1] The index is made up of six footprints (carbon, forest, grazing, fishing, cropland, built-up environment) and compared to "biocapacity," the total regenerative capacity available to serve the demand represented by the footprint. (The ecological footprint represents demand for resources while the biocapacity represents the availability of resources.) Both are expressed in units called global hectares (gha), with 1 gha representing the productive capacity of one hectare of land at world average productivity. The overall result of the indicator is a clear overshoot that has been going on for more than forty years: 1.5 Earths would be required to meet the demands humanity currently makes on the biosphere.

The key message conveyed by the ecological footprint is accurate: the main responsibility for global ecological damage lies with the

TABLE 12.1. Comparing countries' footprints
and economic development levels, 2011

Income Group	Population (millions)	Total ecological footprint	Total biocapacity	Biocapacity (deficit) or reserve	Number of Earths required
World	6,997,990	2,650	1,720	−.930	1,540
Low income (LI)	8,24,850	973	1,124	151	566
Lower-middle income (LM)	2,479,160	1,113	839	−.274	647
Upper-middle income (UM)	2,532,450	2,600	2,286	−.314	1,512
High income (HI)	1,100,180	5,113	3,025	−2,088	2,973

Source: Global Footprint Network.

developed countries, whose patterns of production and consumption, combined with their level of affluence, result in a biocapacity deficit that is the main driver of the global deficit (table 12.1). Developed countries can thus be seen as preempting the development space that should—as discussed in chapter 11—be allocated fairly among the world's countries. Mahatma Gandhi famously asked: "It took Britain half the resources of this planet to achieve its prosperity. How many planets will India require for development?" The answer given by the ecological footprint is that Britain and the developed countries now require almost three planets, while India and all the other emerging countries require a planet and a half.

Yet, the ecological footprint suffers from important limitations. It is far from being a pure physical indicator of pressure on the environment. Its aggregation rules are problematic. It is not global in the sense that it does not account for natural material flows between countries. It is also not socially differentiated. But most of all, much of the information it conveys about national contributions to nonsustainability is embedded in a simpler indicator: the carbon footprint.

The carbon footprint, indeed, accounts for more than half of the total ecological footprint and is the largest single component for more than half of the countries tracked. While the global ecological footprint in 1961 was 7.6 billion gha, it grew to 18.5 in 2011, with the

TABLE 12.2. Global ecological footprint per capita, 1961–2011

	1961	1970	1980	1990	2000	2011
Global	2.4	2.8	2.8	2.7	2.5	2.8
Carbon footprint	0.3	0.9	1.1	1.2	1.2	1.5
Cropland footprint	1.1	1.0	0.8	0.7	0.6	0.6
Grazing footprint	0.4	0.3	0.3	0.2	0.2	0.2
Forest product footprint	0.4	0.4	0.4	0.3	0.3	0.3
Fish footprint	0.1	0.1	0.1	0.1	0.1	0.1
Built-up land	0.1	0.1	0.1	0.1	0.1	0.1

Source: Global Footprint Network.

global biocapacity in the same period growing from 9.7 to 12. If we break down this ever-expanding ecological footprint since 1961, we see that all of the overshoot comes from carbon. (See table 12.2.) Actually, without the carbon footprint, there would be a global biocapacity reserve of 0.5 gha per capita. Surprisingly, all other footprints have either declined (cropland, grazing, forest product) or stagnated (fish, built-up land), pointing to the fact that population has increased even more during the period than the global intake of natural resources. But this relative stability masks absolute declines: the constancy of the fish footprint, for instance, is quite difficult to square with another metric produced by the WWF, the Living Planet Index, or the worrisome reports from the Food and Agriculture Organization of the United Nations on the general situation of world fish stocks.

While the most important piece of information brought by the ecological footprint is the overshoot of the carbon footprint, climate models are more useful purveyors of accurate indicators because they are truly dynamic and allow us to understand in great detail where the emissions come from and what policy instruments can be mobilized to mitigate climate change.[2]

The question of policy is at the center of one of the first comprehensive indicators of environmental performance, the Environmental Sustainability Index (ESI), first developed at Yale and Columbia Universities in 2005 as a "measure of overall progress towards environmental sustainability."[3] This offers data for 146 countries and provides a composite profile of national environmental stewardship based on a compilation of twenty-one indicators derived from seventy-six underlying datasets.

The 2014 Environmental Performance Index (EPI), following up on the ESI, ranked 178 countries on twenty-two performance indicators in ten policy categories and two overarching objectives: ecosystem vitality and environmental health. Its aim was to assess how close a particular country was to an identified policy target, a high-performance benchmark defined primarily by international or national policy goals or established scientific thresholds. (The benchmarks for protected areas were determined through international policy targets established by the CBD.) The scores were then converted to a scale of 0 to 100 by simple arithmetic calculation, with 0 being the farthest from the target and 100 the closest. Comparing the top-ranked country (Finland), China (ranked 109th), and India (141st) helps us to understand that the difference in environmental performance between developed and emerging countries is due to much better environmental health, which brings us back to the importance of social-ecological indicators (figure 12.1).

In the same policy vein, an environmental democracy index (EDI) was recently proposed by the World Resource Institute.[4] It relies on the idea that environmental democracy is enabled by the right and ability of the public to freely access relevant and timely information, provide input and scrutiny into decision making, and challenge before an accessible, independent, and fair legal authority decisions made by public or private actors that may harm the environment or violate their rights. EDI measures the degree to which countries have enacted legally binding rules that provide for environmental information collection and disclosure, public participation across a range of environmental decisions, and fair, affordable, and independent avenues for seeking justice and challenging decisions that affect the environment. Comparing China, India, and the USA allows us to see, for example, that environmental democracy is much more developed in India than in China, but that both lag behind the United States.

These dashboards are quite useful to accurately inform policy. But is it possible to bring together well-being and environmental performance to make progress toward the measurement of sustainability? That was the question asked by economists William Nordhaus and

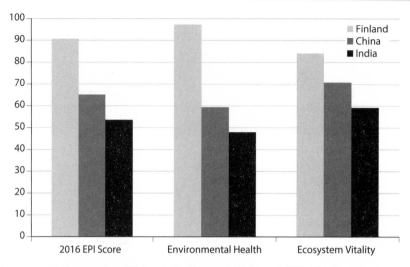

FIGURE 12.1. Comparing Finland, India, and China on EPI 2016 components (indexed from 0 to 100). *Source*: 2016 EPI Data Files.

James Tobin when they proposed a Measured Economic Welfare (MEW) indicator in 1972. This first attempt was picked up by Herman Daly and John Cobb who, in 1989, designed the Index of Sustainable Economic Welfare (ISEW). Their method was full cost accounting, meaning that their indicator accounted not only for market transactions but also for income inequality, non-market benefits, and costs such as voluntary labor and environmental degradation. This has been further refined in the form of a Genuine Progress Indicator (GPI), which can be calculated at the global level and for individual countries. It is especially interesting to contrast the GPI's value and dynamic with that of GDP. In a study spanning 1950 to 2003, global GPI per capita and GDP per capita produced a similar trend for almost three decades, but around 1978, the GPI per capita leveled off and began to decrease slightly, while GDP per capita continued to increase, the same being true at the country level for European countries, China, and the United States.[5] Another way to put it is to say that, globally, GPI per capita does not increase beyond a GDP per capita of around $6,500. In these results, we again encounter the idea of a diminishing return of growth on well-being past a certain point.

TABLE 12.3. Oregon GDP and GPI for 2010, in 2000 million dollars

2010 Oregon GDP (expenditure-based)	133,381
Personal consumption expenditures adjusted for income distribution	−71,024
Total additional beneficial output	+38,458
Total deleterious/unfortunate output	−61,621
GPI (net beneficial output)	= 47,861

Source: I. Kubiszewski, R. Costanza, N. E. Gorko, M. A. Weisdorf, et al. "Estimates of the Genuine Progress Indicator (GPI) for Oregon from 1960-2010 and Recommendations for a Comprehensive Shareholder's Report," *Ecological Economics* 119 (2015): 1–7.

This metric can also be used to improve policy at the local level. A recent illustration shows that, while the US state of Oregon can boast a GDP of $133 million, once this is corrected to account for income inequality, additional beneficial output unaccounted for by GDP (such as the value of volunteer work), and deleterious/unfortunate output (such as the cost of crime), the figure finally translates into a GPI of $47 million (table 12.3).[6]

The major problems of the GPI index and methodology are the relevance and accuracy of its monetization methods. For instance, it relies on the Bureau of Justice Statistics National Crime Survey year-to-year estimates to calculate the cost of crime to victims in terms of their out-of-pocket expenditures or the value of stolen property; these are not exact enough to measure crime's toll on people's well-being. Its aggregation methodology, similar to the one used for the ecological footprint and the EPI, is also a serious limitation: using arithmetical aggregation is equivalent to implicitly assuming perfect substitutability between the components of a given indicator. Alternative methods such as geometric aggregation can yield more accurate results.

The Human Development Index was revised in 2010 on precisely these grounds. As noted by the United Nations,

Poor performance in any dimension is directly reflected in the geometric mean. That is to say, a low achievement in one dimension is not [sic] anymore linearly compensated for by high achievement in another dimension. The geometric mean reduces the level of substitutability between dimensions and at the same time ensures that a 1 percent decline in index of, say, life expectancy has the same impact on the HDI as a 1 percent decline in education or income index. Thus, as a basis for comparisons of achievements, this method is also more respectful of the intrinsic differences across the dimensions than a simple average.[7]

Finally, while the GPI seems to be dynamic, it is not a sustainability indicator. In the words of its designers: "GPI is not meant to be an indicator of sustainability. It is a measure of economic welfare that needs to be viewed alongside biophysical and other indicators. In the end, since one only knows if a system is sustainable after the fact, there can be no direct indicators of sustainability, only predictors."[8] This latter statement is, in fact, debatable, as we will see in the next chapter: imperfect but gradually improving true sustainability indicators are currently being developed at the frontier of research.

FOCUS: HAS CHINA REALLY BECOME THE WORLD'S
LEADING ECONOMIC POWER?

In December 2014, the International Monetary Fund published new data suggesting that China had overtaken the United States to become the world's largest economy. The IMF figures put China's GDP, adjusted for purchasing power parity, at $17.6 trillion, a notch above the USA's $17.4 trillion. Yet, when new indicators of well-being and sustainability are used, the picture changes dramatically.

To begin with, the size of the Chinese economy tells us very little of the actual economic well-being of Chinese citizens. To account for that, we need a demographic criterion and income inequality indicators. These reveal that the per capita income in China is not only about ten times that of Sweden, for example, because of the relative abundance of mouths to feed, but that income is also twice as unevenly distributed. Once this double adjustment is made, China finds itself far behind developed countries.

Regarding human well-being, in such critical dimensions for development as health and education, China is significantly

(continued)

(continued)

behind the group of the most advanced nations, in the middle range of the world's countries according to the UN Human Development Index. Subjective happiness indicators relegate China to about the same rank. When the focus is broadened to consider social progress, including the decisive issue of civil liberties and political rights, the situation appears even more degraded: China is among the 5 percent of the least-free countries in the world, and its situation has deteriorated relative to other nations in the last ten years, all the while economic growth was becoming exponential.

Finally and perhaps more importantly, when sustainable development is considered, the massive environmental degradation that has taken place in China since the early 1990s casts serious doubt on the longevity of the new "first economic power."

China's Ranking According to Several Indicators

Dimension	Metric	Ranking
Size of the economy	GDP in PPP (2014)	1
Standard of living	GDP per capita (2013)	121
Distribution of national income	Income inequality (Gini Index 2013)	120
Human development	HDI = Income + Health + Education (2013)	91
Happiness	Life satisfaction (WHR 2014)	93
Democracy	Voice and accountability (Governance Matters 2014)	170
Environmental quality	EPI 2014	120

CHAPTER 13

Sustainability

It can be said that environmental economics has gone through three stages. The first was centered on resource analysis, and efficient management of scarce renewable or nonrenewable resources was its core objective.[1] The second focused on externality analysis, or how to lower pollution in the biosphere by internalizing externalities.[2] In our own age, environmental economics is closer to ecological economics and is concerned with sustainability analysis/science and attempts to answer the question of what conditions we need to maintain our current level of well-being for future periods or future generations under the existing ecological constraint.

In the broader sense, sustainability is related to sustainable development, a notion that was made widely known by the Brundtland Commission, which defined it as "development that meets the needs of the present without compromising the ability of future generations to meet their own needs."[3] This is a very interesting definition, crossing two dimensions: intragenerational or synchronic justice (poor humans versus the rich humans of today) and intergenerational or diachronic justice (the humans of today versus the humans of tomorrow). However, it appears difficult to operationalize its vision.

Robert Solow, the founding father of modern growth theory, put forward his own practical vision of sustainable development and, by doing so, opened the way for empirical endeavors in the field of sustainability. Sustainability, he wrote in 1993, is the possibility given to the next generation "to achieve a standard of living at least as good as our own and to look after their next generation similarly . . . We are not to consume humanity's capital, in the broadest sense."[4] In other words, we should not deplete the overall stock of capital and overconsume it so that the possibilities for future generations are diminished. (This capital approach to sustainability was first proposed by David Pearce, Anil Markandya, and Edward B. Barbier in 1989.[5])

If we take this perspective, what kind of information should we have in order to make the right policy choices? We should know the current stock of capital(s), the limit/threshold of its depletion, and the desired capital mix for each generation. We should also know what degree of substitution exists between the different forms of capital. We thus need truly dynamic indicators. But this analysis should be global, as our economies and societies are open ones between which capital(s) flows more or less freely. Furthermore, the question is not exclusively about assessing the sustainability of each country taken separately; the problem is a global one for key environmental dimensions such as climate change. Finally, sustainability analysis should be biophysically bounded: the resources of the biosphere are limited and they ultimately determine the possibilities of human development. Therefore, in an ideal world, three dimensions of sustainability analysis are required: dynamic, global, and bounded. Needless to say, we don't have dynamic, global, and bounded indicators. What we do have are imperfect indicators that are very much works in progress. The best ones rely on what can be called a sustainability analysis toolbox, which contains what is needed to build and improve robust sustainability indicators.

But, before moving to practical definitions of both capital and time for our purpose, we need to discuss briefly the relevance of sustainability analysis, understood in Solow's sense of tracking capital in time in a stock and flow perspective. (This means, inter alia, that stocks should not be conflated with flows, as in Lars Osberg and Andrew Sharpe's framework.[6]) Can we legitimately use what is essentially a financial framework to understand and assess sustainability? Many people within the economic profession and even more outside of it dispute this. Two fundamental arguments have been articulated against such an approach, the first that notions such as "social capital" or "human capital" are more evocative metaphors than robust notions, the second that reasoning in capital terms eventually implies the monetization of dimensions of well-being that cannot or should not be monetized (such as ecosystems, for fear that monetization leads to commodification and eventually marketization).

Let's try to answer these two arguments. Regarding the first one, made mostly by economists, it is no small paradox that two of the most prominent voices to have sharply criticized the use of the concept of capital in reference to trust, education, and health have both played an important role in disseminating an approach to sustainability that relies on a stock and flow framework.[7] Solow has taken issue with the use of social capital, contending that this was "an attempt to gain conviction from a bad analogy."[8] Kenneth Arrow argued in 1999 against not only social capital but also the concept of human capital. In his view, capital properly defined along the lines of manufactured capital has three properties: extension in time, deliberate sacrifice for future benefit, and alienability (that is, transferable from one person to another). By 2015, he had changed and refined this typology a bit, arguing that capital should (1) be productive, meaning that increasing the amount of it should increase the production of goods; (2) constitute a store of value to the owner; and finally (3) be alienable.[9]

If one is to consider the first typology, while social and human capital can be said to extend in time, for Arrow (1999) they do not imply either sacrifice for future benefits or alienability. If one is to adopt the second typology, for Arrow (2015), human capital satisfies conditions 1 and 2 but not 3. Other economists have disagreed more or less sharply with these views,[10] while Arrow himself, in various seminal works where human capital, health capital, and intangible capital are mobilized to assess "the multitude of capital assets the economy has inherited from the past," now seems to harbor a more positive view of measuring comprehensive wealth via the aggregation of different facets of capital.[11]

Considering the definition of Robert Putnam, according to whom social capital is made up of "networks and the associated norms of reciprocity and trustworthiness" that arise from such networks, there are in fact strong reasons to believe that social capital is indeed capital, and even a critical form of it. Because social capital differs from manufactured capital does not imply that it should not be treated as capital. Elinor Ostrom has noted that social capital is indeed different from other forms of capital in four ways: (1) use and disuse (social capital depreciates by disuse); (2) it is not easy to see and measure; (3) it is hard to build from outside; and (4) institutions play a key role. Social capital can thus be understood as a public good in which societies tend to underinvest. If capital can be defined as crystallized labor that can be used over time for development and can be created and destroyed, social capital can be thought of as crystallized collective labor that fosters social cooperation and can be either built or broken. What is more, accumulating social capital allows societies to build or preserve other forms of capital through efficient reform. This kind of capital is rightly recognized as an essential element for the success of the Nordic countries.

The same can be said of human capital, understood as the quantity and quality of human populations. The accumulation of an important "stock" of population is a key determinant of the long-term development of societies, while health is also cumulative, via genetics and human practices. Considered at the collective level (national or communal), both social and human capital can be said to extend in time, imply a sacrifice—they require policies that increase health, education, or good institutions, and these are costly—and be transferable from generation to generation. A number of indicators reviewed in the previous chapters can actually be used to quantify both human capital and social capital.

The second argument posits that founding sustainability analysis on the concept of capital reflects an economic vision of the world and implies a risk of monetization of everything human. Some authors, such as French sociologist Dominique Méda, have recommended using the more neutral notion of "heritage" in the sense of UNESCO, an organization that inventories the world's most remarkable cultural assets. But this concept is more retrospective than prospective. It is also not true that measuring capital necessarily means monetization or marketization. A simple example is provided by the concept of carbon budget that was used in chapter 11.

The carbon budget can be understood as an indicator of the carbon capital that humans share, yet it is not measured in monetary units but in gigatons of carbon. If governments chose to implement a carbon tax in order to slow and eventually bring carbon emissions to zero, thereby preserving humanity's carbon capital by putting a price on the element, then this carbon budget would be translated in monetary units. This would actually be highly desirable. Other climate change mitigation policies, such as norms and standards, do not imply monetization. Hence, to quantify natural capital does not inevitably mean monetizing or marketing it. What is more, there is a difference between putting a price on scarce resources and turning those resources into commodities. All commodities have prices, but not all things with prices are commodities. To continue with the example of climate-change mitigation policy, there is a difference between a carbon tax and a cap-and-trade system in which permits are given free to polluters and therefore are tradeable. Both put a price on the limited carbon-absorptive capacity of the atmosphere. But the former does not make this into a commodity, while the latter does.

Monetary approaches have been developed to assess natural capital. The System of Environmental-Economic Accounting (SEEA), which contains the internationally agreed-upon standard concepts, definitions, classifications, accounting rules, and tables for producing internationally comparable statistics on the environment and its relationship with the economy, is an example of natural capital monetization (although the accounts are also expressed in physical units). The SEEA framework follows a similar accounting structure as the System of National Accounts, but the latter's accounts are called "satellite" accounts, which suggests that environmental concerns still take a back seat to economic development. Yet, natural capital is best understood not as a set of fixed assets, but rather as a consistent ensemble of interrelated dynamic processes in which humans play a major role and whose functions should be maintained for their own good. This is the meaning of preserving ecosystemic services such as water purification or climate regulation.

It thus seems fully relevant to engage in sustainability analysis equipped with the concept of capital in a stock and flow framework. Multidimensional well-being is a flow resulting from the stock of several forms of capital. Capital is essentially crystallized labor that must not be reconstituted every day so that the labor can be used for something else. (Capital is labor-saving or, alternatively, leisure-augmenting.) It can be understood as the sum of human wealth, the overall stock of assets accumulated by humans in the last seven million years, passed on from generation to generation, and distributed unequally among countries and groups. Humans are more or less commonly responsible for these assets, and overconsumption of them results in a depletion that lowers the well-being benefits for current and future generations. Accounting for this overall stock of capital in order to track its depletion is of vital importance.

Since the seminal article by Solow, this analytical framework has been implicitly used, either wholly or partially, in empirical studies by the World Bank and the OECD and numerous journal articles, but it has not been formalized. In their 2016 book *Pursuing Sustainability*, Pamela Matson, William C. Clark, and Krister Andersson provided, for the first time, a fully-fledged model of sustainability analysis "à la Solow." After asserting that "development is sustainable if inclusive social well-being does not decline over multiple generations," they state that "well-being is ultimately grounded on five clusters of underlying capital assets" and carefully define them (table 13.1). The key insight here is that the real issue is not the relevance of the concept of capital for sustainability analysis, but the scope of the capital considered in the analysis. It is unconvincing to simply restrict the study of capital in the early twenty-first century to manufactured capital, as Thomas Piketty (2014) does.[12] Capital can take at least five different forms, all of which are more or less easily measurable and more or less tangible.[13]

Of course, this redefinition of capital can easily be criticized as just another extension of the logic of capitalism. On the contrary, reclaiming capital could be one of the most profound reforms of the capitalist system. After all, the etymology of capital is *capita* (head), or the main part of a loan as opposed to its interests. In other words, capital should be what matters the most.

One can obviously not rely on market prices to properly evaluate all these assets. Another instrument must thus be added to the sustainability toolbox when capital assets are considered: shadow prices. As explained by Partha Dasgupta, "Formally, by an asset's shadow price, we mean the net increase in societal well-being that would be enjoyed if an additional unit of that asset were made available, other things being equal. As shadow prices reflect the social scarcities of capital assets, it is only in exceptional circumstances that they equal market prices."[14] One important dimension of this societal value is that we

TABLE 13.1. Capital in the twenty-first century

Type of capital, from most to least measurable	Components
Manufactured capital (tangible)	Industrial system (factories, roads, cities, infrastructure, etc.) and financial systems (stock markets, bond markets, etc.)
Human capital (intangible)	Population, health, education
Social capital (tangible and intangible)	Arrangements (economic, political, cultural) governing interactions (rules, norms, trust, networks) and institutions (courts, parliaments, etc.)
Knowledge capital (intangible)	Scientific findings, technology, practical skills and expertise
Natural capital (tangible)	Environmental system, its ecology, ecosystems, climate, soils, biodiversity, minerals, etc.

Source: Author, adapted from Matson, Clark and Andersson (2016).

need to determine the value of capital through time, for current but also future generations, which calls for a third instrument in relation to time: discount rates.

Taking time into account amounts to answering the following question: what is the value of capital today given all the income flows derived from capital in the future? This is the basic question of private investment, which answers with the following formula: present value = future value / $(1 + r)$ n, where r is the interest rate and n is the number of periods of time (years, for instance). The reason why cost-benefit analysis must have a time dimension is what economists call the "depreciation of the future": individuals have a "time preference" that makes them prefer an amount today to the promise of the same amount in the future. It is therefore necessary to convert future amounts into their current equivalents or to discount them, which is none other than the familiar compound interest calculation, but in reverse. Over periods of fifty years, which are common in environmental policy assessments, the choice of a discount rate that differs by a few percentage points from another yields widely different costs and benefits: $100 at an annual discount rate of 4 percent amounts to only $14 after fifty years, while it amounts to $37 at a 2 percent rate, $60 at a 1 percent rate, and $95 at a 0.1 percent rate.

When this calculation involves private decisions, such as real estate investments, it is customary to choose a value near the interest rate observed in the market, since the alternative would be to place the sum in a bank or invest in the stock market at this rate. But how to choose the discount rate applicable to public decisions? Economist Frank Ramsey proposed in the 1920s a breakdown of the different components of what is now referred to as the social discount rate. He wrote that the social discount rate R (sometimes called the "social rate of time preference") was equal to $p + (e \times g)$, with p as the pure rate of time preference (a rate of impatience of present generations to consume), e as an intergenerational inequality aversion parameter, and g as the growth rate of per capita consumption. We can thus choose "our common future" by selecting the values of the different parameters of the social discount rate.

The danger of this discounting instrument is clear: whenever one looks at costs occurring at dates far enough apart in time, choosing a positive social discount rate value, even a very low one, minimizes the costs of our decisions for future generations and maximizes benefits closer in time. In spite of their limitations, social discount rates are the most important instruments of the sustainability toolbox and are widely used, for instance in climate-change models. The latest IPCC Assessment Report has presented the different options chosen by scholars over the years, which imply different choices of parameters (table 13.2).

The controversy surrounding the UK's *Stern Review on the Economics of Climate Change*, initially published in 2006, which attempted to assess the costs and benefits of climate policies, showed exactly how the choice of the social discount rate was decisive in the evaluation of climate mitigation costs and efforts. This report offered a striking evaluation of the economic consequences of climate change by estimating that by 2050, it would cost 1 percent of global GDP every year to stabilize greenhouse gas CO_2 equivalent emissions between 500 and 550 parts per million. The potential cost of inaction would range between 5 and 20 percent of world GDP every year. The cost of inaction appeared far greater than the cost of action.

TABLE 13.2. Calibration of the discount rate based on the Ramsey rule

Authors	% rate of pure preference for present	Inequality aversion	Anticipated growth rate (%)	Implied social discount rate (%)
Cline (1992)	0.0	1.5	1.0	1.5
IPCC (1996)	0.0	1.5–2.0	1.6–8.0	2.4–16.0
Arrow (1999)	0.0	2.0	2.0	4.0
UK: Green Book (HM Treasury, 2003)	1.5	1.0	2.0	3.5*
US UMB (2003)	—	—	—	3.0–7.0
France: Rapport Lebègue (2005)	0.0	2.0	2	4.0*
Stern (2007)	0.1	1.0	1.3	1.4
Arrow (2007)	—	2.0–3.0	—	—
Dasgupta (2007)	0.1	2.0–4.0	—	—
Weitzman (2007)	2.0	2.0	2.0	6.0
Nordhaus (2008)	1.0	2.0	2.0	5.0

*Decreasing with the time horizon.

Source: IPCC 2014.

However, the *Stern Review*'s evaluation of the social discount rate and its components seemed to depart from the existing literature. Richard Tol, for instance, felt that the report's findings were "alarmist," if not totally "incompetent."[15] In contrast, Martin Weitzman attempted to validate Stern's approach by claiming that there was indeed wide scientific uncertainty as to the magnitude and effects of climate change, insofar as unknown consequences existed whose impact could be extreme. Because uncertainty was high, it was right that the discount rate was indeed very low.[16]

Whatever the economic and normative justification behind the choice of the different parameters that constitute the social discount rate, it should be noted that it implies widely different outcomes because of the very long time frame when environmental issues are considered. As argued above, applying a discount rate of 4 percent yields a monetary evaluation of benefits or costs that appear to be one-seventh the original after fifty years. The lower the social discount rate, the higher our efforts should be today; the higher the rate, the higher the burden for future generations.

Relying on our definitions of capital and social discounting, we can now make progress toward sustainability assessment. Let's first consider a paradox. GDP is produced by mobilizing assets that are largely invisible in national accounts. If GDP is truly the income return on wealth (the flow to a stock), then it is clear that this wealth must be much greater than only manufactured capital. (The US GDP is currently as high as $16 trillion.) The intuition here is that "missing assets" not included in the standard measure of capital should be included and valued appropriately. Growth accounting was indeed at the heart of modern growth theory and empirics: in exogenous growth theory such as that developed by Solow in 1956 and 1957, total factor productivity was the mysterious "residual" (the share of growth not explained by increase in factors' quantity). In the same way, well-being accounting lies at the basis of sustainability theory and empirics. When attempts are made to estimate the comprehensive wealth of nations, it appears that the reason rich nations are rich is not because of manufactured or financial capital; an assessment of all its dimensions shows that their wealth is made of human capital at 50 to 80 percent (table 13.3). Conversely, natural capital constitutes a much more important share of lower-income nations; as countries become more economically developed, the share of intangible capital in their overall wealth increases and the share of their natural capital decreases.

So, can we build a robust indicator of comprehensive wealth to track it in time? The two most convincing attempts so far in this direction have been the adjusted net savings (ANS) and the inclusive wealth index (IWI). The ANS, which was developed by the World Bank, attempts to measure "the true rate of savings in an economy after taking into account investment in human capital, depletion of natural resources, and damage caused by pollution."[17] It is calculated as the net national savings in the economy plus education expenditure and minus natural resource depletion (the sum of energy depletion, mineral depletion, and net forest depletion) and carbon dioxide and particulate emissions damage. We can, for instance, compare OECD countries, the most-developed on the planet, with the sub-Saharan countries; these

TABLE 13.3. The comprehensive wealth of nations, in $ per capita and %, 2010

	Total wealth	Intangible capital	%	Produced capital	%	Natural capital	%
Low income	6,523	3,469	53	945	14	2,316	36
Lower-middle income	17,112	8,675	51	4,130	24	4,357	25
Upper-middle income	84,844	57,777	68	14,309	17	14,104	17
High income: OECD	581,424	473,799	81	98,561	17	10,946	2
World	115,484	88,361	77	20,329	18	7,119	6

Source: World Bank.

TABLE 13.4. ANS for OECD and sub-Saharan countries, 2012 (% of GNI)

	OECD	Sub-Saharan Africa
Adjusted savings: gross savings	20.2	23.8
Adjusted savings: net national savings	3.6	14.8
Adjusted savings: education expenditure	4.7	3.7
Adjusted savings: natural resources depletion	1.0	11.4
Adjusted savings: particulate emission damage	0.1	0.8
Adjusted savings: carbon dioxide damage	0.3	0.5
Adjusted net savings, excluding particulate emission damage	7.0	6.6
Adjusted net savings, including particulate emission damage	6.9	5.8

Source: World Bank.

include some of the least-developed countries, but they are fast developing according to ANS (table 13.4).

The surprise here comes from the fact that these countries have almost the same overall rate of savings (6 to 7 percent). But the reasons for this are different and this is when this indicator becomes really interesting. Africa's net national savings are much higher because capital there is newer and consumption of fixed capital is much higher in the OECD. Education expenditure is a bit higher in the OECD. But the big rebalancing comes from the depletion of natural resources. The cost of pollution is also higher in Africa. In all, the OECD saves a bit more than Africa.

There are many possible policy applications of ANS. One of them is to devise a development strategy based on the conversion of natural capital into human capital. In countries that strongly rely on this source of income, for instance, nonsustainability can be due to insufficient reinvestment of income generated by the extraction of fossil resources into education, so this indicator is an interesting take on development strategy for countries with high natural capital. But ANS also has important limitations: at best, it represents sustainability's economic component and, because there are no physical boundaries in its calculation, cannot be understood as an indication of environmental or ecological sustainability. Similarly, it relies on a weak definition of sustainability whereby infinite substitution of natural capital by other forms of capital is possible, which is highly unlikely. Finally, ANS is not global; its results change significantly when carbon trade is included.

An attempt to improve ANS is being undertaken by the authors of the IWI, the latest version of which covers 140 countries. IWI is calculated as the sum of social value of manufactured capital, to which is added the social value of human capital and the social value of natural capital. (Social value means that the indicator uses a shadow price and discounting.) Natural capital is composed of fossil fuels (oil, natural gas, coal), minerals (bauxite, nickel, copper, phosphate, gold), timber forest resources, non-timber forest resources, and agricultural land. Human capital includes education and health. Produced capital is composed of equipment, machineries, and roads and other infrastructures.

Many interesting lessons can be drawn from the IWI data, starting with the nature of wealth. Produced capital, the type for which by far the most exhaustive and reliable data exist, represents only about 18 percent of the total wealth of nations. The remaining capital types together constitute 82 percent of wealth, 54 percent in human capital and 28 percent in natural capital. In high-income countries, almost two-thirds of the wealth comes from human capital alone (table 13.5).

On average, human capital contributes 55 percent of overall gains in inclusive wealth, produced capital 32 percent, and natural capital 13 percent. But the global dynamic to which this indicator points is worrisome. Population growth and natural capital depreciation are the main drivers of declining wealth per capita in the majority of countries.

TABLE 13.5. The true wealth of nations (1990–2010 average, in %)

	Human capital	Produced capital	Natural capital
High income	64	24	12
Low income	47	12	41
Lower-middle income	46	15	39
Upper-middle income	55	19	25
Total world average	54	18	28

Source: IWR 2014.

Natural capital declined in 90 percent of the 140 countries. Overall, while GDP per capita has increased by 50 percent since 1990, IWI per capita has increased by a mere 3 percent. The study's authors conclude that "countries striving to improve their citizens' well-being—and to do so sustainably—should reorient economic policy planning and evaluation away from targeting GDP growth as a primary objective and toward incorporating inclusive wealth accounting as part of a sustainable development agenda."[18]

To conclude this chapter, we can represent the relation between well-being, where we started this book, and comprehensive wealth, the indicator closer to sustainability assessment, in a simple diagram adapted from Pamela Matson, William C. Clark, and Krister Andersson's *Pursuing Sustainability* (figure 13.1). There are two differences in this representation from the formal framework put forward by the authors, which, again, is the first model to detail the intuition of Solow. The first is that the constituents of well-being considered are not broken down the same, although they largely overlap; the more important second factor is that processes of distribution of both wealth (stock) and well-being (flow) have been added to account for the importance of inequality and the concern for economic, social, and environmental justice, all through the formation of human well-being.

These new indicators' future evolution, given their focus on changes in existing wealth stocks, undeniably represents progress in the knowledge and assessment of sustainability. However, they are only a first step in the right direction and their shortcomings are many. It is especially in the choice of evaluation of human capital and total factor

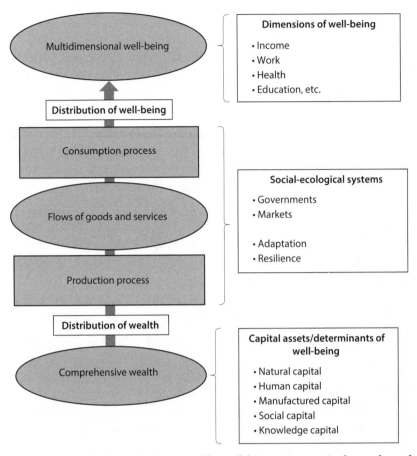

FIGURE 13.1. The dynamic of sustainable well-being. *Source*: Author, adapted from Pamela Matson, William C. Clark, and Krister Andersson, *Pursuing Sustainability: A Guide to the Science and Practice* (Princeton, NJ: Princeton University Press, 2016).

productivity that their methodology seems most questionable: the market returns to education are the basis for assessing the education dimension of human capital, and the health dimension is based on a valuation of the life expectancy that, too, rests on monetary gains. These methods are therefore at least partly inconsistent with the analysis developed in the chapters of this book devoted to the relevant measurements of education and health.

Further, one of the main objections raised by the assessment of sustainability using a single indicator is the aggregation process of the different components of this stock, which implies that they are perfectly and indefinitely substitutable: one euro or dollar of accumulated productive capital or human capital compensates one euro or dollar lost in natural capital. According to this view, if the world population continues to increase, provided it is sufficiently educated, the current process of economic development is eminently sustainable, to the extent that the stock of wealth bequeathed to future generations is also increasing, although its natural component could be reduced to a trickle.[19]

Can we reasonably assume substitutability without boundary between the different components of real wealth of stock at the global level or that of a country? We can, to some extent, substitute manufactured capital for natural capital, thanks to technological advances: Europe has certainly massively reduced the size of its forests since the Middle Ages, and who would think to complain that cities and arable fields have replaced them? Similarly, small states in the Middle East are actively preparing for the post-oil era by investing their natural capital in human capital. There are many possibilities for substitution, and they are even more extensive than our current skills and knowledge. But this substitution cannot be continued without limit or risk. In theory, it is quite possible to build indicators of sustainability based on the concept of comprehensive wealth; by attributing adequate "shadow prices," the price of each component of the overall stock of capital will rise enough when this item becomes rarer. But will we one day know how to accurately evaluate these rarities, and will we have the political will to react accordingly to these price increases?

It is neither reasonable nor politically and morally defensible to opt for strong sustainability, which means preserving at any price the natural environment and existing ecosystems, even sacrificing opportunities for people whose basic needs are not met today. But if weak sustainability gives us hope that the world we leave to future generations will be livable, it casts uncertainty over the ability of current and future humans to manage the risks that it carries, and gives no guarantee that the world of tomorrow will be desirable. In other words, the well-being and sustainability transition cannot be reduced to its technical dimension: as part III of this book will discuss, it is a democratic matter.

FOCUS: FROM DEVELOPMENT GOALS TO SUSTAINABLE
DEVELOPMENT GOALS[20]

The Sustainable Development Goals (SDGs) were adopted as
the cornerstone of the 2030 United Nations Agenda for Sustainable Development on September 25, 2015, in New York. The set
of seventeen SDGs, supported by 169 targets, aim, inter alia,
at ending poverty, fighting inequality, and tackling climate
change. They came into effect on January 1, 2016, and are intended to guide the actions and decisions of world leaders for
the following fifteen years at all levels of governance.

The UN adopted the Sustainable Development Goals fifteen years after the Millennium Development Goals (MDGs),
which ranged from halving extreme poverty rates to halting the
spread of HIV/AIDS and providing universal primary education, all by the target date of 2015. The new agenda aims to build
on the MDGs and complete the goals that were not achieved,
while also going beyond them to set a range of economic, social,
and environmental objectives.

In the words of the new agenda, "sustainable development
recognizes that eradicating poverty in all its forms and dimensions, combatting inequality within and among countries, preserving the planet, creating sustained, inclusive, and sustainable economic growth and fostering social inclusion are linked
to each other and are interdependent."[21]

Sustainable Development Goals:

Goal 1. End poverty in all its forms everywhere

Goal 2. End hunger, achieve food security and improved nutrition, and promote sustainable agriculture

Goal 3. Ensure healthy lives and promote well-being for all at
all ages

Goal 4. Ensure inclusive and equitable quality education and
promote lifelong learning opportunities for all

Goal 5. Achieve gender equality and empower all women and
girls

Goal 6. Ensure availability and sustainable management of
water and sanitation for all

(continued)

(continued)

Goal 7. Ensure access to affordable, reliable, sustainable, and modern energy for all

Goal 8. Promote sustained, inclusive, and sustainable economic growth, full and productive employment, and decent work for all

Goal 9. Build resilient infrastructure, promote inclusive and sustainable industrialization, and foster innovation

Goal 10. Reduce inequality within and among countries

Goal 11. Make cities and human settlements inclusive, safe, resilient, and sustainable

Goal 12. Ensure sustainable consumption and production patterns

Goal 13. Take urgent action to combat climate change and its impacts

Goal 14. Conserve and sustainably use the oceans, seas, and marine resources for sustainable development

Goal 15. Protect, restore, and promote sustainable use of terrestrial ecosystems, sustainably manage forests, combat desertification, and halt and reverse land degradation and halt biodiversity loss

Goal 16. Promote peaceful and inclusive societies for sustainable development, provide access to justice for all, and build effective, accountable, and inclusive institutions at all levels

Goal 17. Strengthen the means of implementation and revitalize the Global Partnership for Sustainable Development

One of the key ideas behind this new agenda was to move from well-being goals to sustainability targets. It is, of course, useful that the countries of the world were able to agree on such a comprehensive approach to development, which acknowledges and represents many of the well-being and sustainability dimensions covered in this book.

Yet, this inventory also suffers from serious limitations. First, there are too many objectives. There are also 140 subindicators beyond the seventeen core indicators, so that priorities are impossible to identify. To be accurate and policy-effective, the

(continued)

(continued)

dashboard should have a limited number of indicators. Despite the goals being broken down into smaller targets, it is still a challenge for nations (and the UN overall) to individually track their progress toward these goals. Further, the different goals seem more juxtaposed than properly articulated; the connection between well-being and sustainability is not really outlined (as, for instance, the obvious relation between goal 1, to eradicate poverty, and goal 13, to combat climate change and alleviate its impact). The fact that increasing economic growth as measured by GDP is considered an objective and quantified on a par with combatting climate change (and thus limiting greenhouse emissions) can also be viewed as a potential contradiction in terms, if not a policy oxymoron. Finally, it is very hard to locate critical trade-offs. This is a common flaw of policy strategies, which are almost always defined in terms of targets and objectives but hardly ever in terms of obstacles and trade-offs. It is impossible to achieve all objectives at the same time and there is inevitably some conflict between them. However, we need to understand what those conflicts of objectives might be in order to deal with them.

The UN Statistical Commission has begun developing a comprehensive official indicator framework for the seventeen SDGs and 169 targets. So far, the Inter-Agency and Expert Group on SDG Indicators (IAEG-SDGs) has identified nearly 230 indicators, an unwieldy number for governments to track and manage. Through the Sustainable Development Network, Jeffrey D. Sachs and his colleagues have proposed an aggregate indicator index utilizing quantitative metrics for each sustainable development goal and normalizing the highly heterogeneous data by assigning each country a percentile rank for each variable measured. This aggregate index would allow for ranking across the SDGs to assess the progress of individual countries relative to their peers. Sachs's group has also introduced an SDG Dashboard that presents the data visually for each goal to highlight that even countries ranked highly on the overall SDG index still face major challenges. While the proposed index and

(continued)

(continued)

dashboard are not official SDG indicators, they represent useful tools for governments to better implement and incorporate these goals into real policy measures, which is the ultimate goal of any good sustainability indicator.

The Quantification of an Aggregate Indicator[22]

$$I_k(N_k, I_{jk}, \rho) = \left[\sum_{j=1}^{N_k} \frac{1}{N_k} I_{jk}^{-\rho} \right]^{-\frac{1}{\rho}}$$

Where:

k = each country

j = each SDG

I_k = aggregate indicator for country k

N_k = number of SDGs available for country k

ρ = substitution parameter (the substitutability across components of the indicator, with a range of $-1 < \rho < \infty$)

PART III

Managing the Well-Being and Sustainability Transition

This book has so far tried to show that many indicators of well-being and sustainability exist that are alternative or complementary to conventional economic indicators, and that these are likely to inform policy makers and the public about the real complexity of our economic world. But how can we change attitudes and behaviors in order to put these new visions into practice?

The following chapters discuss three critical issues in relation to this challenge. The first is the question of the principles underlying the well-being and sustainability transition, that is to say the values that must be mobilized to rethink our economic world. The second relates to how to go about this collective enterprise, which must employ methods that are democratic in the fullest sense of the word. The last relates to the kinds of institutions necessary to carry this social transformation forward, particularly the key role to be played by local jurisdictions as vectors of the transition. Principles, methods, institutions: such is the triptych of transition.

CHAPTER 14

Valuing What Counts

The ability to change human societies depends on two key levers: the behaviors and the attitudes of their members. Behaviors are triggered by economic and other signals that people perceive (or do not perceive) and that they choose (or do not choose) to respond to. Inertia is thus a form of behavior that can result from the non-collection of a signal or the inability or lack of will to respond to it.

A concrete example of behavioral signal and response can be found in the reaction to the rising price of tobacco in recent decades. This has induced a decrease in the average volume of tobacco consumed in the EU and the United States (where consumption of cigarettes has been more than halved from its historical peak of 1980, while the price of a pack has increased by a factor of six). Reducing cigarette consumption in response to a price increase does not necessarily imply adherence to the preventive health message that is the justification for the increase from the point of view of the public authorities. Putting unbearable photographs of lesions caused by smoking-induced cancer on a pack made a few dollars more expensive, however, is intended precisely to encourage such adherence, by playing on the fear and shame of the consumer. The hope is that such a vivid representation of the consequences of smoking will change the way the smoker thinks about his or her own consumption and make cigarettes no longer desirable at the individual or social level. This social aspect is particularly important with young smokers. The idea is that the policy both appeals to the individual's value system and alters the system of economic incentives. If it works, people will buy fewer cigarettes because they are convinced that it is bad for their health or that of others, and that belief will out-weigh any consideration of pleasure, fun, or "coolness."

We instinctively understand that this second mechanism is going to be more powerful and durable than the financial disincentives. While higher prices can be seen as a temporary constraint to which consum-ers can refuse to submit or that they can try to get around (by, for in-stance, cutting back on other consumptions), the change in values is a personal choice that is often, in the case of tobacco, definitive. People will stop smoking because they believe it is socially unacceptable or bad for their health, not just because it is bad for their wallet.

The introduction and use of new indicators of well-being and sus-tainability fall under the same logic of policy efficiency: the aim is not to impose new measurement instruments to institutions, organi-zations, and ultimately people so that they more or less gracefully comply, but to convince members of society that this reform will be beneficial and thus trigger a change in attitudes, not just behaviors. The transition in behaviors is actually already taking place under one powerful driver: need.

In the summer of 2014, at the height of a drought that had lasted for three years in California and proved summer after summer to be the most serious for more than a century, the *San Francisco Chronicle* pub-lished a cartoon in two vignettes: The first, taking place in 1894 at the peak of the region's gold rush, shows a prospector leaning toward the river and peering feverishly at his pan to exclaim, "Gold!" The second, dated 2014, shows the exact same scene with the same character in the same position, this time exclaiming, "Water!" What has fundamentally changed in over a century is that the drought has made water more precious than gold. This story is not unlike that of King Midas, who was granted by Dionysus his request to be able to change anything he touched into gold. Midas soon realized he could no longer drink or eat, and begged the god to make him human again.

The gold-and-water parable teaches us that value is not forever fixed; it is fundamentally a social construct that varies according to historical circumstances. For Midas, gold suddenly becomes a curse when he realizes that his gift deprives him of common abilities. For Californians, water will soon be the most precious asset, worth literally millions of dollars. Behaviors are already changing in the region, but it may be a case of too little too late to preserve the region's ecosystems and secure the human presence in this land of plenty.

While the transition in incentives is already under way, we need to prioritize well-being and sustainability over short-sighted economic development measured by GDP growth by favoring a transition in values. For that, we first need to realize that we cannot rely on so-called free markets. The current situation in the market for fossil fuels makes this point very clearly. The price of oil, which suddenly dropped dramatically between 2014 and 2015, has become a powerful brake on the development of renewable energy and energy transition, even though they are becoming more competitive each year. The markets are impeding the energy transition they are supposed to naturally promote. The explanation is simple: global demand collapsed in 2014, largely as a result of China's economic slowdown; on the supply side, OPEC refused to cut production (Saudi Arabia, OPEC's leader, was engaged in a double standoff with the United States, both on the issue of shale oils, which compete with conventional oil, and the reversal of the Obama administration's sanctions on Iran, which had been allowed to reenter the global market.) The price has therefore collapsed, dragging down the profitability of many sectors of the green economy, including renewable energy. The agreement reached within OPEC at the end of 2016 has not fundamentally changed this dynamic.

The geopolitical issues at play behind oil markets' dynamics worldwide are not negligible, but they are unrelated to climate change, which exceeds them all in importance. Clearly, we cannot rely on the oil market to produce the price signal that will mitigate the climate crisis. We need public authorities to fix markets by assuming their responsibility to determine prices according to values.

Another fossil-energy market that is largely dysfunctional from an ecological point of view is the one for coal. The colossal consumption by emerging countries (especially China, but increasingly India) of this major source of greenhouse gas emissions has made it the top global polluter. But here, also, its low price does not reflect the high environmental and health costs with which it is associated. Without resolute public action to price coal in accordance with the ecological and human health damage it does, coal production and consumption will continue to harm locally and globally, causing death and illness for millions of Asians and aggravating the climate crisis instead of helping to solve it.

This transition of values may take many decades to be fully realized, but it won't happen by the magic of markets. It is currently blocked by three major obstacles: ideas, interests, and institutions. Economic instruments controlled by public authorities can be powerful allies in overcoming some obstacles and bringing about change both in behaviors and attitudes. Putting a price on carbon means harnessing the power of markets to make them work for the transition to low carbon; altering patterns in production, consumption, housing, transport, and the like; and gradually reducing the role of fossil fuels in the economic system. But that change in incentives must be accompanied by an awareness that leads people to opt for low-carbon solutions because they are convinced of their multiple benefits and not just because they are constrained by the price system. This brings us to an essential point: we cannot advocate and promote the well-being and sustainability transition using the language of standard economics and the rationale of growth.

Indeed, it makes little sense to call for an economic system that would value health as a fundamental dimension of human well-being because it would lead to more economic growth, or to condemn inequality because it lowers GDP, or to engage citizens in reducing pollution because doing so would mean more profits. This way of going beyond GDP only to come back to it illustrates the difference between a revolution and a roundabout. Health is important in itself, not because it would allow faster economic growth, in the same way that democracy matters because of the benefits it brings to individuals and not because it makes them more productive. Doing away with pollution should be valued for its effects on human health, not accounted for in additional GDP points. We should develop an intrinsic rather than an instrumental approach to well-being and sustainability; in other words, these must become the ultimate goals of policy making and not intermediate targets toward growth. There will be no real transition of values if growth remains the *ultima ratio* of social cooperation. To paraphrase Albert Einstein, if we continue to have a hammer-shaped mind, we will continue to see a world populated by nails.

A key distinction should be made here among quantification, monetization, and commodification (or marketization). This book certainly argues for quantification of the invisible value so that it is not ignored or blindly destroyed. This is the example of health or trust. But this quantification should not necessarily imply monetization. After all, we argued in chapter 5 against giving a price to life using VSL. And this monetization, when necessary, does not lead inevitably to commodification, as in the example of carbon tax vs cap-and-trade in climate-change mitigation.

Some well-being dimensions, such as friendly or romantic relationships or spirituality, should not be subject to quantification regardless of their obvious importance to people's well-being. However, social networks can be valuable for an individual and their usefulness should be quantified in order to highlight their importance in policy making and enable the government to identify shortcomings in this area and, if necessary, address them. This is particularly important in relation to catastrophic events such as tsunamis, heat waves, and floods because people are better able to deal with them if they are supported by a large, strong social network. But there is no need at all to monetize its value. The example of Bhutan (chapter 7) shows that it also makes sense to quantify the quality of cultural attachments, again without monetizing them.

Monetization should also be approached with care. The need for monetization stems from a legitimate concern: how to convince decision makers and citizens of the need to change without showing them what a new economic world can bring to them in comparison to the old one. How can the benefits of transition be made tangible without speaking the language of standard economics? As Marc Fleurbaey and Didier Blanchet rightly remark, "putting a price on everything is not a promising way of going beyond GDP."[1] In fact, monetization can sometimes be useful, as we have seen with the local management of ecosystem services, but it is often impossible and sometimes dangerous. And it can be merely meaningless.

One example in which monetization becomes impossible is attempting to assign a monetary value to human life. Because money does not have the same meaning and the same value from one human being to another, seeking to gauge an individual's desire to protect life or health from their "willingness to pay" is logically bound to fail. As we have seen, the quality of human life can be measured accurately without using a monetary unit. Monetization also becomes dangerous when natural resources are priced according to the needs and interests of a handful of people without involving all the stakeholders, including the powerless and future generations. Meaningless monetization takes place when the physical limits of the biosphere are translated into monetary metrics, as, for instance, when the severity of ecological crises is assessed by the loss of GDP they will incur. Knowing that GDP would be reduced by 50 percent in a 6°C warmer world, where life would be essentially a nightmare, is neither useful information nor a leverage for change.

The danger of commodification is obvious when considering natural resources, but it is also problematic when education or housing become areas of fierce competition for the acquisition of so-called positional goods, whose value depends on their position relative to others (what Fred Hirsch identified in his 1977 book of the same name as the "social limits to growth"). What is more, the creation of monetary value can lead to the destruction of social values. A well-known example taken from the social psychology literature deserves to be recalled here briefly. Imagine a day-care center where some of the parents are occasionally late to pick up their beloved toddlers. Exasperated by this inconsiderate behavior, which means the staff have to wait for late-comers before they can close the facility, the management establishes a system of fines depending on the gravity of the delay. The result is that delays increase instead of declining. One possible explanation for this apparent social paradox is that the introduction of monetary value has destroyed the moral values that led the vast majority of parents to respect the school schedule. By establishing a correspondence between irresponsible behavior and financial penalties, the school management has taken out punctuality from the values system and brought it into the economic system. In the latter, being late becomes an option because it is the subject of a payment. Value destroys values.

Attempting to alter values in order to change behaviors and attitudes is thus not without risk, but it is indispensable for a simple reason: we live in a world where many dimensions of human well-being already have a value and often a price; it is the pluralism of value that can therefore protect those dimensions from the dictatorship of the single price. For instance, revealing the invisible value of health amounts to protecting it. The case of food, already mentioned, is particularly telling: if the only dimension of food resources that receives recognition is their economic cost, the health dimension will never be reflected in production and/or consumption behavior. Appropriate labelling, on the other hand, will inform the consumer about important aspects of the food that manufacturers may have an interest in concealing, such as the presence of chemical additives, the total caloric value, or its salt or fat content.

To destroy a wetland rich in biodiversity on the basis of the economic value of the housing that can be built on it is to rely on one value (the immediate economic one) against all the others that have just as much bearing on human well-being. Revealing the plural values of biodiversity or ecosystems, monetized or not, amounts in this case to protecting them from blind destruction. Broadening the range of values taken into consideration opens up at the same time the range of behaviors and attitudes that will gradually build the well-being and sustainability transition.

But can we really believe in the possibility of transition? Aren't the ideas, interests, and institutions preventing it stronger than ever, starting with the power of standard economic models over the political mindset?

First, as we have seen, the power of necessity should not be underestimated: human behaviors can change abruptly when circumstances dictate. The two oil shocks of 1973 and 1978 are good examples of such sudden shifts. At that time, in the Western world, the rising cost of energy led to the adoption of all-out savings measures, especially in housing and transportation, the most spectacular in many European countries being a reinstituted World War I time change that lasts up to today. Can one imagine a more disruptive and traumatic change than to turn back the whole human system an hour by pure convention with the avowed aim of saving a scarce resource? We cannot say with certainty that attitudes concerning energy have changed over the years since this measure was adopted, but behaviors undeniably have.

It is simply untrue that our societies are resistant to change, automatically driven by immutable behaviors and attitudes. Human societies have not ceased to change according to new values. The most powerful drivers of the well-being and sustainability transition are political in the best sense. We must build institutions that embody the principles of well-being and sustainability and use new indicators to prove that this transition is beneficial for citizens. Contradictory and sometimes challenging dialogues will be necessary, but we can count on the most effective political system we know to bring about this dialogue: the democratic regime, whose defining quality is to constantly question itself and whose greatest power is to be able to change course and correct its mistakes. This is why this book will now turn to the ways in which citizens can engage in the well-being and sustainability transition.

CHAPTER 15

Engaging Citizens

As was noted in the introduction, new indicators of well-being and sustainability are entering an unfamiliar phase: the challenge is not just to interpret or even analyze the economic world, but to change it. We thus need to understand how new indicators can become performative. This does not depend only on the technical quality of the new metrics, but, much more importantly, on their becoming embedded in public debate and the democratic process.

Let's start with the state of the public debate in economics, where a lot of progress has already been made. When people talk about economics nowadays the conversation tends to be populated with those indicators that dominate commentary in both the media and politics, often without debate. At the heart of contemporary concerns in the developed world we find a "mystic square" formed by stock market performance, the levels of deficit and public debt, and GDP growth. None of these indicators is directly related to well-being, let alone sustainability; at best, they are intermediate targets that policy makers hope will contribute indirectly to human development. (The impact on sustainability is rarely, if ever, envisioned.)

What is more, this mystic square is used in a monomaniac way: it is always good that stock markets increase, regardless of the risks of financial crisis that such an increase may mean; it is always healthy to reduce deficits (irrespective of the business cycle) and contain the debt (regardless of cost-effectiveness of public investment); more GDP growth is always good news, regardless of its actual impact on the welfare of people and the damage it can cause to sustainability of societies.

The first priority must be to de-pollute the economic debate in order to make way for a plural approach to well-being and introduce complexity into this set of false economic compasses. Each economic indicator should be accompanied by at least one other indicator. This is the very meaning of the concept of economic system: it is impossible to assess an economic indicator without reference to at least one other, whose function is to qualify it. It is impossible to assess the real meaning of GDP growth in the United States without knowing how this creation of economic wealth is being distributed among citizens, or to comment on growth in China without understanding how the country's ecosystems are being affected by it.

The question of the periodicity of economic data is also central. The fact that stock market indicators are discussed several times a day on regular news programs and all day long on specialist financial channels and websites gives them a disproportionate weight in the assessment of the economic situation, even though they are unrelated to the welfare of the vast majority of citizens and quite misleading regarding the state of the real economy. There is, indeed, no reason to conclude or to open the news with the figures from the stock markets, except to emphasize that financial markets are the most important thing in our economic world, a highly debatable notion. Because they are readily available and abundant, financial data have become the most used and commented-upon indicators and have taken center stage in the public debate in economics, although they are in reality extremely short-term and arcane.

As I noted in the introduction, the defining qualities of economic indicators are that they be purposeful and policy-relevant but also democratically contestable; in other words, they can be understood and debated by ordinary citizens. This can be done in three important ways: through representative democracy, regulatory democracy, and democratic activism.

Much can be achieved via legislative action. One important reform is including indicators of well-being and sustainability in parliamentary debates and decisions, since Parliament (or its US equivalent, Congress) is historically the site of political deliberation and action in democratic regimes. A first step, undertaken in France in 2015, may be to provide a list of alternative indicators to members of Parliament when they vote on the budget in order to enrich their economic understanding.[1] It should be possible in coming years to create in France and other OECD countries permanent independent parliamentary bodies modeled after the Congressional Budget Office (CBO), in charge of disseminating alternative economic indicators.[2] The CBO is arguably one of the best institutions for public policy evaluation in the world, but it very much relies on standard economic models and indicators.

One 2015 report produced by the CBO is telling in this respect: it predicts that the abolition of the Affordable Care Act (also known as "Obamacare") would increase GDP growth by increasing the supply of labor and estimates this increased growth potential to be 0.7 percent over the period 2021–2025.[3] In other words, abolishing a health insurance made available to fifteen million Americans would worsen their quality of life from the point of view of their health and leisure/family life, but this would be good for growth because it would require the newly uninsured to work more in order to finance their health coverage.

The aim should therefore be to reinvent public policy evaluation by creating a parliamentary body in OECD countries that could become a place of continuing deliberation on public choice impacting well-being and sustainability, where experts are able to mobilize the right indicators on the right issues and provide policy makers with the relevant information to make their choices. In other words, these new institutions could foster a new parliamentary culture of well-being and sustainability.

The second reform concerns regulatory democracy and, more precisely, the reform of economic instruments used routinely by the executive branch of the government to design public policies once laws have been adopted. Public policies today too often rely on simplistic models framed by cost-benefit analysis (CBA). CBA evaluates the efficiency (and profitability) of a project by calculating the net worth or net benefits it produces, that is, the amount of potential benefit less the costs associated with the project. The only dimensions to enter the analysis are economic flows (benefits and costs) that can be monetized. We can see immediately that cost-benefit analysis translated to the micro level follows the same philosophy and thus suffers from the same limitations and flaws that GDP does at the macro level. Among the typical omissions of cost-benefit analysis we usually find nonmonetary costs/benefits to human health and nonmonetary costs/benefits of the impact on ecosystems. Here again at play is the key difference already noted between cost-effectiveness and neoclassical "efficiency": the former is about means; the latter awards economics the more ambitious task of defining ends. It is much more interesting to replace these methods with a multicriteria analysis where the financial cost or benefit is not the sole reference and where intangible effects are considered alongside tangible ones—or at least to perform sensitivity tests to evaluate the impact of alternative parameters, especially social discount rates, on CBA results.

If economic analysis can indeed be usefully mobilized to illuminate a project, it is important to provide policy makers with a comprehensive cost-benefit analysis of at least two possible projects and compare the results to nonstandard economic approaches. The assessment of public and private project practices must therefore be made more plural; otherwise, the most immediate dimension of economic well-being will prevail over all the others, possibly damaging not only current but also future well-being. This damage might take decades to grasp and could eventually be impossible to repair.

Participatory democracy must strengthen these reforms of governmental action. Democracy is not just one dimension of well-being, but also the method that must govern its definition. It is at once an outcome and an input. Many participatory tools exist, such as investigations performed within the SPIRAL method designed to bring out the essential elements of well-being from direct dialogues between citizens, and also between citizens and experts, as in the case of "citizens' conferences."[4] The typical setting would include a panel of citizens, experts, and decision makers discussing the respective importance of different dimensions of well-being and agreeing on a common dashboard implemented at the local level. (This will be discussed in the next chapter.)

This leads us finally to consider the role democratic activism can play in engaging citizens in the well-being and sustainability transition. Ecological economist Joan Martinez-Alier has shown that what he calls "ecological distribution conflicts"—social conflicts that relate to the distribution of natural resources and pollution—are fruitful ways to open up a public debate on the different values assigned to the use of natural resources.[5]

A key argument is the idea that the costs of natural resource extraction, transportation, and consumption, which have greatly intensified and are generating a huge amount of pollution and waste, are, first and foremost, assumed by the poorest and most vulnerable populations. From this results a counterintuitive fact: that environmentalism is not a luxury but a necessity, and, as such, a daily condition for the survival of the most disadvantaged people on every continent. The poor are concerned about their environment because they are the first victims of degradation and they alert the rest of society to the reality of the current crisis. An example of this is the inhabitants of the Pacific Islands alerting the world to the speed of the rising oceans and seas as a result of climate change. This is why there has long been a "spontaneous environmentalism of the poor." It results in subtracting natural resources from the commercial sphere and revealing the plurality of their values beyond monetary benefits.

In other words, conflicts over natural resources used around the world, from the Keystone XL pipeline to Lake Chad, are also conflicts about values and valuation and, as such, help citizens to better understand the complexity of our economic world. The recent student activism in major US universities on the need to divest from fossil fuels is emblematic of the usefulness of these valuation controversies. But for citizens' engagement to become really powerful, it needs an institutional anchor, and it is precisely here that local jurisdictions come into play.

CHAPTER 16

Building Tangible and Resilient Transitions

There are two strong reasons why local jurisdictions (cities, metropolitan areas, regions), even more than the nation-states, can become vectors of the well-being and sustainability transition. The first is their renewed power and influence under the combined impact of globalization and urbanization. The regions are not administrative subdivisions any more, but rather autonomous multipliers of development: every policy is now local. Actually, in the last two decades, economic globalization has given birth to a paradox. On the one hand, what some have called the "death of distance" has been driven by the falling cost of transport, energy, and communication, while new technologies have made long-distance trade easier and barriers have continued to fall or be lowered. On the other hand, the localization of economic activity matters more and more and has begun to shape our economic world, both in theory and reality. In this new era, regions have made a noticeable comeback.

Since the early 1990s the new economic geography has developed new models in which distance is the code of economic activity.[1] Here, trade-offs between transport costs and economies of scale (due to increasing returns in human interactions) determine where production should be localized. Urban economics, whose basic intuition is the need to consider housing and transportation costs together, not separately, has refined these intuitions at the household level and shown that economic decisions such as housing are also shaped by spatial factors. Space-driven decisions—the main variables of which are concentration of employment, the presence of social and cultural amenities, the price of land, cost and size of housing, and travel costs—explain, in the words of Jan Brueckner, "why cities exist" and how they evolve.[2]

A city is, in economic terms, a place of efficient agglomeration of jobs, goods, services, people, and ideas. When its size increases, the benefits of economic, social, and nonmarket amenities that the city can provide also increase. But the price of housing and costs related to congestion swell. Urban sprawl can be one response to this costly dynamic by lowering housing prices or increasing the amount of available housing. This spread, in turn, increases the distance between home and employment (or place of study or leisure) and thus constrains mobility. The result is a trade-off for individuals between the costs of housing and transportation, which results in the determination of their preferred social/spatial location.

The spatial distribution of consumption and production is thus the result of conflicting centrifugal and centripetal forces that lead firms and households to concentrate and disperse according to preferences and incentives. Space has become the key for understanding economic dynamics.

Paralleling this analytical effort and driving it, in the last two decades regions have become powerful economic actors, emerging alongside well-identified and widely studied institutions such as firms and nation-states. The combination of accelerating globalization and urbanization had led to the advent of a "local era" where the two driving forces together allowed the regions to concentrate population, economic wealth, and employment in an unprecedented way at the global level, reminiscent of the reign of European city-states in the Middle Ages. While almost 70 percent of the OECD population currently lives in urban areas, the 275 metropolitan areas located in these countries now account for 48 percent of the organization's population and 49 percent of its employment.

Because all OECD countries have witnessed the phenomenon of growing concentration of human and physical capital, accounting for the "reign of space," geographic disparities have become greater than in the past. Indeed, spatial disparity results much more in our world from human geography than from physical. The new economic geography has labelled disparities resulting from economic activity inequalities of "second nature."[3] First-nature inequalities are differences between regions resulting from environmental conditions (climate, sea access, mountain relief, etc.). As the product of physical geography, they are "exogenous" in the sense that humans are not responsible for them and can hardly do away with them. (They can, however, domesticate them by overcoming some of their most adverse consequences, as with agriculture in Saudi Arabia.) Second-nature inequalities are not the product of natural conditions but of human factors driving economic development, chief among them the division of labor, commercial and financial integration, and the dissemination of technical progress, that is, the combination of institutions and integration that explains long-term divergence between and within nations.

One easy way to visualize first-nature inequalities between regions is to observe the planet or a given country by day: mountains and rivers are not evenly distributed over the physical space and create substantially different economic opportunities for residents of regions with different physical geographic endowments. But inequalities of second nature are more clearly visible by night, such as the bright lights of urban areas that dot the surface of the planet and signal economic concentration. The striking contrast in satellite photos released by NASA between the visibility of the major areas of economic activity worldwide and the darkness of areas of lesser economic concentration reveals how much our globalization has become spatially uneven. The World Bank was indeed right to stress that, in our world, "place is the most important correlate of a person's welfare."[4]

To better understand the crucial importance of local conditions in framing personal well-being, let's consider two countries that find themselves at the two extremes of the OECD employment rate distribution: Canada, with the highest employment rate, and Italy, with the lowest. Comparing these two nations seems to make good economic sense to determine in which "place" individuals have the best opportunity to find work. Yet, regional differences within both countries, measured by the employment rate, are actually greater than the difference between them at the national level. Without a regional assessment of employment rates, it is actually quite difficult to accurately assess the access to employment that individuals experience in their daily life.[5]

The implication of this simple example is straightforward for the measurement of individual well-being: because in our era regional contrasts and disparities are often stronger than national ones, we lose precious information on the well-being experienced by individuals by averaging regional values at the national level. Well-being is best measured where it is actually experienced. Accurately measuring local well-being gaps also has a political importance: as many recent elections have shown from the UK to the United States, France, and Italy, not living in the same well-being space means not living in the same political space. Not living in the same area implies not living in the same era.

To sum up, we live in a "local era" shaped by a "reign of space" that determines substantial differences between localities within each country. In this era, regional and local governments have important responsibilities for most of the policies that relate most directly to people's lives. They are important to the extent that they provide services that enhance economic dynamism and represent the bulk of public investment. About 40 percent of all public expenditure in the OECD is made at the regional and municipal level of government; 70 percent of this local public spending concerns education, health, social protection, and public services in general. Local levels of government thus have a substantial and immediate impact on the well-being of the population. In addition, most interactions between different public policies are specific to territories. Land use, transportation, and housing, for example, differ between locations, and interactions between these strands of public policy can be genuinely understood and managed where they occur.

Hence, measuring well-being at the local level can help decision makers prioritize public intervention where it is most needed to better assess and control the spatial concentration of benefits or difficulties and improve consistency by identifying synergies between policy dimensions. In other words, regions are more agile than states, not to mention international institutions, and better able to put in motion well-being indicators and translate them into new policies. We can talk, in this respect, after the late Elinor Ostrom, of a "polycentric transition," meaning that each level of government can seize the opportunity of the well-being and sustainability transition without waiting for the impetus to come from above. We now need a theoretical framework to fully understand the importance of space when it comes to assessing individual well-being.

As we saw in chapter 3, Amartya Sen's conception of justice is concerned with concrete situations of inequality or located injustice. In addition, the capability approach recognizes as an object of justice not just material conditions such as income, but also real possibilities given to individuals to live the life they have reasons to value. The capability approach thus recommends that well-being be assessed beyond material conditions and reflects also the quality of life of a given person, as the broader measure of human development purports to do. It is thus the adequate framework for studying and measuring well-being at the local level, where it is effectively experienced. How can we apply this capability approach to local well-being?

We first have to show that location matters for the well-being of individuals, because it determines the scope of opportunities and options they can choose from in order to live the life they value. It is important in this respect to understand a given area as an institution, in the sense stated by Douglass North (a "humanly devised constraint that structures social interactions").[6] It is also important to understand in this respect that there is no conflict between people and place. Localities, like institutions, determine the possibilities of their inhabitants' existence; they mediate their individual freedom, which is partly bounded by the institutional framework defined by their jurisdiction. A place, in the language of Sen, can be a multiplier or a divider of people's capabilities and function: geography, in great part, determines history.

The key is therefore not to oppose individual well-being and territorial well-being, but to explore their interconnectedness. Individuals' well-being is place-based, in the sense that it is determined by factors linked to their physical location. Outcomes are shaped by a combination of place-based factors and the individuals' characteristics. This is true for both material living conditions and quality-of-life dimensions, whether objective or subjective (figure 16.1).

The OECD project "How's Life in Your Region?" applies this analytical framework to local well-being at the level of metropolitan areas and regions.[7] It focuses both on individuals and the specific characteristics of the locality. The selected indicators measure outcomes rather than the resources invested (or inputs). Table 16.1 presents the set of comparable indicators that now exist for 362 regions in thirty-four OECD countries.

	Place-based factors	$+$ Individual characteristics	$=$ Individual outcomes
Material living conditions Income and jobs	Dynamism of regional economic context, regional labor pool, access to training, transports, information networks	Family, education, skills, motivation	Employment, household net adjusted disposable income per person, average gross annual earnings of full-time employees
Quality of life (objective) Health	Social conditions (housing, heating, relative and absolute inequality, etc.); environmental conditions (pollution, amenities, etc.)	Biological and genetic factors, life style, risky behaviors, income	Life expectancy at birth
Quality of life (subjective) Happiness	Access to amenities, noise, pollution, community life and support, economic conditions, security	Mental health/ psychological resilience, family and personal life, character	Life satisfaction

FIGURE 16.1. People in places: place-based well-being. *Source*: Author.

Because the indicators are normalized and aggregated on a relative scale from 0 to 10, based on the values of all regions, they enable a direct comparison between well-being dimensions over time. It is also possible to compare well-being in each region to that in the other 361 OECD regions.

The study's results indicate clearly that unaccounted-for regional differences can bias international comparisons. For instance, the Île-de-France region (around the city of Paris) is among the top 20 percent of OECD regions in terms of health, while another French region, the Nord-Pas-de-Calais, is among the last 50 percent. The difference in life expectancy between the two regions is four and a half years (Île-de-France, eighty-four years, and Nord-Pas-de-Calais, seventy-nine and a half years). This corresponds to roughly half of the nine-year difference

TABLE 16.1. Measuring local well-being

	Topics	Indicators
Material conditions		
	Income	Household disposable income per capita (in real USD PPP)
	Jobs	Employment rate (%)
		Unemployment rate (%)
	Housing	Number of rooms per person (ratio)
	Health	Life expectancy at birth (years)
		Age-adjusted mortality rate (per 1,000 people)
	Education	Share of labor force with at least secondary education (%)
Quality of life		
	Environment	Estimated average exposure to air pollution in PM2.5
	Safety	Homicide rate (per 100,000 people)
	Civic engagement	Voter turnout (%)
	Accessibility of services	Share of households with broadband access (%)

Source: OECD. See also Monica Brezzi, Luiz de Mello, and Éloi Laurent. "Au-delà du PIB, en-deçà du PIB: Mesurer le bien-être territorial dans l'OCDE," *Revue de l'OFCE* 145 (2016): 11–32.

between Japan, the OECD country with the highest age score, and Mexico, which has the lowest. In the United States, the Gini coefficient of household income in the District of Columbia (0.48) has about the same value as that of Mexico, while the level of inequality in Iowa (0.32) is similar to that of France.

Such a framework encourages thinking in an integrated way about all dimensions of well-being. Most interactions between these dimensions are relevant locally. For example, in metropolitan areas effective active labor market policies may require improving access to public transport and the supply of housing, which help to improve the standard of living and social equality. An integrated approach that measures the impact of each dimension on the other can help to develop coherent policy responses, prioritize areas of public intervention and alignment across all sectors and levels of government, and provide a common vision of the progress of society.

Several interesting initiatives have been undertaken in recent years to assess well-being at the regional level from various perspectives using different methodologies and data.[8] They all show why, at the local level, it is important to go "beyond GDP," but also beyond national averages (or "beneath GDP").

The first insight of place-based well-being might be to show that, on a given dimension of well-being, a microapproach yields more accurate result than a macro one, be it national or regional. This is precisely the angle of the Small Area Methods for Poverty and Living Condition Estimates (SAMPLE) project, developed from 2008 to 2011 under the auspices of the European Commission to identify alternative indicators to assess poverty and inequality and focusing on the microterritorial level, at LAU1 and LAU2 (the first two levels of local administrative unit).[9] The project was clearly policy-oriented, aiming to provide "a dashboard of reliable indicators of poverty and deprivation defined at NUTS3, NUTS4 level [Nomenclature of Territorial Units for Statistics regions of Europe], useful for Local Government Agencies" in order to help them "ensure monitoring of poverty and inequality" and "focus their policies on segments of population at higher risk of poverty, some of them especially elusive."

One important insight from the Italian case study of the SAMPLE project is that the nation's traditional north-south divide should be complemented and refined by substantial intraregional differences. The southern region Campania does not only experience higher levels of poverty and inequality than its northern neighbors, but also more dispersed ones. The analytical insight here is that regionally refined data help us understand more clearly the social dynamics underlying regional contrasts and better focus local public policy. Furthermore, it is clear that it is not only the national level that can be deceptive but also the regional one: intraregional difference is sometimes worth exploring when contrasts are important.

Yet this microapproach is also limited because only one dimension of well-being is considered here, capturing only a fraction of well-being outcomes. The questions of data availability for the other dimensions, as well as their comparability, immediately come to mind when considering the generalization of such approaches.

A broader approach to place-based well-being is provided by studies focusing on human development through a tridimensional composite index approach encompassing living standards/income, education, and health, and following more or less closely the methodology used by the United Nations in its Human Development Report since the early 1990s. In the United States, Measure of America has adapted the UN methodology for territories and used it to provide human development metrics for states, metro areas, and counties.[10] The basic insight from this approach is that the US geographical distribution of well-being varies widely: the average index value is around 5, but top-ranked Connecticut reaches 6.17, or more than one and a half times the level reached by Mississippi, at the bottom of the ranking. (See figure 16.2.)

The human development gap may seem low, but it is actually almost equivalent to the gap between the United States as a whole and the African island nation of São Tomé and Principe, respectively ranked third and 156th in the Human Development Index by the United Nations. National averages are misleading indeed.

More striking still is the observation of substantial human development gaps within the same metropolitan area. Los Angeles is well situated, on average, within the United States and even the state of California when it comes to human development, but the gap between its most- and least-developed areas reaches a factor of 4.6. In the early 2010s, the least-developed areas experienced levels of human development that the United States as a whole had achieved by the mid-1960s. In other words, this spatial study of well-being reveals that people in areas distant by only a few kilometers evolve in different worlds of human development. We find this kind of difference in cities such as New York, where the fourteenth district, located on the Upper East Side, one of the most privileged parts of Manhattan, and the sixteenth district, located in the Bronx, are separated by the equivalent of fifty years of human development but are only 3.5 km (2.17 miles) and five subway stations apart.

The data compiled by Measure of America make it possible to link the regional perspective with two other dimensions: race/ethnicity and

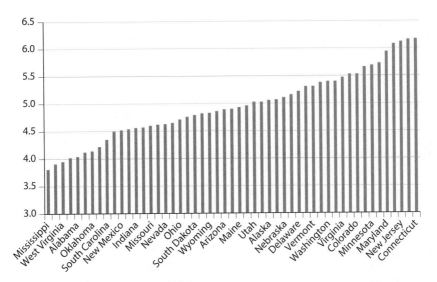

FIGURE 16.2. Human development index in US states, on a scale from 0 to 10.
Source: Measure of America.

gender. One possible limitation of these data is the absence of systematic comparison with GDP, although the authors develop their index explicitly as an alternative to it. (There is, however, a comparison between the historical evolution of GDP and HDI in the United States, showing that while gross domestic product increased from $3.1 trillion to $14.5 trillion, or +362 percent, between 1960 and 2010, HDI increased by only 209 percent, from 1.63 to 5.03, during the same period.) Another limitation is the fact that the Human Development Index used, like its UN model, comprises only three, albeit essential, dimensions of well-being.

In a similar human development vein, the Direction générale de la prospective of the Nord-Pas-de-Calais region in the North of France has developed a methodology ranking the twenty-two French metropolitan regions according to GDP per capita on the one hand and on the other according to an adapted version of the HDI, the HDI-2, a tridimensional index composed of disposable median income by consumption unit, life expectancy at birth, and the percentage of residents over age fifteen without a high-school degree.[11] The HDI approach can be said to bring some added value to the GDP perspective (table 16.2). Furthermore, using these data, one can gain a sense of comparison between production logic on the one hand and quality of life on the other, pointing to regional specialization. Yet, one can see that the HDI is not the exact opposite of GDP per capita, which means that regional specialization is not clear-cut between productive regions and residential regions. One can also compare the income and non-income components of HDI-2 and GDP per capita to test whether the latter is a good proxy of household income and HDI, the high correlation between HDI and GDP per capita often being a subject of criticism. This correlation is actually weak in the case of France, so that HDI-2 really brings something new into assessing well-being beyond GDP. Finally, one can compare ranking according to the different components of human development and see where the difference between regions is made.

The study was extended to introduce a broader composite index of well-being, the Index of Social Health (ISH), which weights measures of income, poverty, education, health, employment, working conditions, housing, and social links. The insight from this broader approach is that the distance between GDP per capita and ISH is even greater than the one between GDP per capita and HDI, and that HDI and ISH correlate only weakly. This indicates the value added by these new dimensions and suggests that the introduction of others, such as environmental conditions, would reflect the full scope of subjective well-being even better (table 16.2).

At the EU level, the regional directorate of the European Commission has conducted a study to compare GDP per capita and HDI for NUTS 2 regions. The main insight here is to go beneath the general picture of a continent where HDI is high for all member states in order to get a better sense of the well-being experienced by European citizens residing in different areas. The authors of the study note in this respect that "despite the very high HDI scores in Europe, there is significant variation between EU countries and regions in terms of human development and poverty" and that "low education attainment in European regions ranges from 3.3% to 81.4%; healthy life expectancy ranges between 52 and 78 years."[12] Here, also, the authors have adapted the HDI index at the regional level using as income component the net adjusted disposable household income per capita as an index of the European Union average to better account for regional differences. A third

TABLE 16.2. French regions according to three different metrics, 2012

Region	GDP per capita (euros)	Rank	HDI-2*	Rank	ISH*	Rank
Île-de-France	47,696	1	0.788	1	48.2	17
Rhône-Alpes	30,513	2	0.763	3	61.8	7
Provence-Alpes-Côte d'Azur	28,500	3	0.735	10	43.9	19
Alsace	28,285	4	0.742	7	65.6	5
Champagne-Ardenne	27,917	5	0.687	20	51.1	16
Haute-Normandie	27,584	6	0.693	18	46.6	18
Pays de la Loire	27,357	7	0.746	6	66.3	3
Aquitaine	27,322	8	0.755	4	60.9	8
Midi-Pyrénées	27,254	9	0.765	2	62.1	6
Bretagne	26,530	10	0.755	5	67.6	2
Bourgogne	26,459	11	0.721	14	57.7	13
Centre	26,449	12	0.736	9	59.1	11
Auvergne	25,260	13	0.735	11	65.9	4
Poitou-Charentes	25,010	14	0.733	13	59.5	10
Franche-Comté	24,908	15	0.733	12	60.5	9
Nord-Pas-de-Calais	24,683	16	0.651	22	33.3	22
Basse-Normandie	24,536	17	0.703	16	58.0	12
Lorraine	24,497	18	0.696	17	53.7	15
Limousin	24,296	19	0.742	8	71.3	1
Picardie	23,872	20	0.664	21	38.4	21
Corse	23,803	21	0.689	19	54.8	14
Languedoc-Roussillon	23,741	22	0.711	15	42.5	20

*See text for definitions.

Source: Direction générale de la prospective du Nord-Pas-de-Calais.

insight is that regional differences are sometimes wider than national differences; for instance, HDI variation within the United Kingdom appears to be greater than the difference between the UK and seventeen other European countries.

A final insight is that the HDI is itself limited in that it does not reflect distributional issues: a region with an unequal distribution of a high level of income can have both a high average level of human development and a high level of poverty. Hence, an even broader approach to well-being than human development is needed.

An alternative to the human development approach involves monetizing the different dimensions that are omitted or minimized by GDP, using the Genuine Progress Index methodology and applying it at the regional level. This is what the Regional Index of Sustainable Economic Well-Being intends to do.[13] As a monetary figure, the R-ISEW can be compared with Gross Value Added (GVA) and other economic indicators the very same way that the GPI can be compared to GDP. The insight here is that well-being is lower than economic indicators suggest, the R-ISEW for England in 2008 being evaluated at £12,111 per capita, or just 42 percent of per capita GVA for the country, which stood at £21,020.

Here, also, the difference between ranking according to traditional economic metrics and well-being metrics is very clear. The authors note, "Whilst London is the region with the largest per capita figure for both (an R-ISEW of £15,097 per capita), it is the South West that has the second highest R-ISEW (£14,454 per capita) despite only having the fourth highest GVA. Meanwhile rich regions such as the South East and the East of England have some of the lowest R-ISEWs."[14] The limitation of this study is the same as that for the GPI framework (see chapter 12), which suffers from many methodological shortcomings due to the monetization choices made for each component and the compound effect of aggregating them.

The subjective approach helps assessment of well-being at the local level using surveys rather than objective data and can thus be tailor-made for a given location and provide much broader and more accurate measurement. However, it suffers from the interpretation, meaning, habituation effect, and other traditional problems associated with subjective data. A first initiative in this methodological category was undertaken by the Australian Centre of Excellence for Local Government, whose *Community Wellbeing Indicators: Measures for Local Government Report* is clearly policy-oriented, intended to assist local councils in better evaluating "the progress of community wellbeing [sic] in their local government areas."[15] Aboriginal Affairs and Northern Development Canada has built a composite Community Well-Being Index out of surveys on well-being in eight domains based on questionnaires, following the methodology of Bhutan. (See the chapter on happiness.) Great Britain undertook a similar effort in its 2013 report *Measuring National Well-Being: Personal Well-Being in the UK.*

The first insight from the UK study is the importance of regional differences: "Among the English regions, the South West and the South East had some of the highest levels of average life satisfaction and worthwhile ratings in 2012/13. The South West also had proportionately more people than any other region rating life satisfaction, worthwhile and happiness as 9 or 10 out of 10."[16] The second insight should be the exploration of the interaction between individual well-being and local context. (The Office for National Statistics has announced that it will publish a further analysis of the local determinants of individual well-being.)

These studies show that we need not only a broad definition of well-being that encompasses subjective as well as objective measures, but also a better understanding of how place determines individual well-being.

A recent US academic project looks precisely at the way local opportunities shape social mobility. Using income data, the Equality of Opportunity Project calculates different measures of intergenerational mobility that it is able to localize, providing a picture of how space impacts social dynamic.[17] The authors of one study built measures of relative and absolute mobility for 741 "commuting zones," geographical aggregations of counties based on commuting patterns that are similar to metro areas but also cover rural areas. They are able to show strong differences between areas, sometimes stronger than international variations (table 16.3). They summarized their findings by noting, "Some cities—such as Salt Lake City and San Jose—have rates of mobility comparable to countries with the highest rates of relative mobility, such as Denmark. Other cities—such as Atlanta and Milwaukee—have lower rates of mobility than any developed country for which data are currently available."[18]

While the mobility measure reported here is biased by differences in economic and employment growth rates among the cities, the key insight from this study remains: that well-being at a given point in time is the result of opportunities given to individuals over time, those opportunities varying significantly from one region to another.

TABLE 16.3. Upward Mobility in the 50 Biggest Cities:
The Top 10 and Bottom 10 in 2012

Ranking		%
1	Seattle	11.6
2	Minneapolis	9.7
3	Salt Lake City	9.2
4	Reading, PA	9.1
5	Madison	7.4
6	Des Moines	6.6
7	Omaha	6.4
8	Washington, DC	5.8
9	Spokane	5.6
10	Portland, OR	5.2
90	Chicago	−11.1
91	Fresno	−11.1
92	Orlando	−11.4
93	Memphis	−11.6
94	Greenville, SC	−12.2
95	Raleigh	−12.6
96	Columbia, SC	−13.9
97	Charlotte, NC	−14.4
98	Greensboro, NC	−14.8
99	New Orleans	−14.8
100	Fayetteville	−17.8

Note: This table shows the percentage gain (or loss) in income from growing up in each of the one hundred largest US commuting zones for children from low-income families (25th percentile). For example, if a child were to grow up in the Seattle metro area instead of an average place, he or she would make about 12 percent more at age twenty-six.

Source: The Equality of Opportunity Project.

These various studies of local well-being converge toward three important points. First, measuring well-being at the local rather than the national level brings important and precious information on individual well-being due to significant interregional differences, oftentimes more important than international disparities. The spatial distribution of well-being thus appears to be a key dimension of the distribution of well-being. Generally speaking, local well-being gives a better sense than national well-being of the actual experience of individuals on the ground. Second, metrics built for the national level have to be adapted to account for the local level. A broad measure is needed; objective and subjective metrics can be combined in assembling it. Finally, because a locality is an institution, understanding how space shapes its social dynamic is important, so that place-based well-being has to be assessed over time and not only at a given moment.

One way to project local well-being in time is to try to define and measure territorial resilience. Local resilience must be understood in the general context of the growing literature on social resilience. The concept of resilience, which is today widespread in scientific research in various disciplines, was born in the fields of physics and psychology and, in the broader sense, means the ability of a system to tolerate a shock and return to equilibrium afterward without changing its fundamental nature. It was applied quite successfully to environmental science: ecological resilience means the ability of ecosystems to absorb shock (natural or human) without an essential change. An ecosystem could survive a shock, but see, for example, its natural productivity drop drastically or some of its functions deteriorate or disappear.

As noted by Charles Perrings, "the concept of resilience has two main variants. One is concerned with the time taken for a disturbed system to return to some initial state . . . a second is concerned with the magnitude of disturbance that can be absorbed before a system flips from one state to another."[19] Ecological resilience and social resilience are obviously linked. According to W. Neil Adger, in the context of social-ecological systems, resilience "refers to the magnitude of disturbance that can be absorbed before a system changes to a radically different state as well as the capacity to self-organise and the capacity for adaptation to emerging circumstances."[20]

Romaine Duval and Lukas Vogel tried to apply the concept to economies and defined "economic resilience" as comprising "at least two dimensions: the extent to which shocks are dampened and the speed with which economies revert to normal following a shock."[21] By the same token, social resilience can be understood as referring to the capacity of human societies to absorb the effects of shocks and learn from them in order to move forward. Michèle Lamont and Peter Hall have greatly contributed to our understanding of the notion of social resilience, showing how people in different societies have tried to lead a good life in the face of economic, social, and cultural changes brought about by the neoliberal turn.[22] Social resilience is of critical importance when analyzing natural risk and disasters. As such, it is a strategic element in the United Nations strategy for disaster risk reduction, where it is defined as "the ability of a system, community or society exposed to hazards to resist, absorb, accommodate to and recover from the effects of a hazard in a timely and efficient manner, including through the preservation and restoration of its essential basic structures and functions."[23]

I understand social resilience as the ability of human societies to collectively bear the effects of environmental shocks (e.g., climate change) and economic stress (e.g., a severe recession, as in 2009) without disintegrating, and to learn from them in order to mitigate future shocks. Residents of Paris are rich in all sorts of ways today, but will they still be, and will they be able to return to their current level of well-being, if their city experiences a centennial flooding of the river Seine, a possibility that many see as a probability?

In fact, the concept of local resilience appears particularly relevant because the effects of shocks are often asymmetrical nationally due to local characteristics and specializations and capacity for heterogeneous response.

Building on these various but convergent definitions to make progress on empirical measures of local resilience, we need to analytically break down the concept of resilience. The literature on natural disasters has defined *vulnerability* as the result of exposure to shock and sensitivity to it, these two elements constituting the potential impact of the disaster on an individual or a community.[24] Local resilience can then be defined as the result of vulnerability and adaptability, where the latter comprises the capacity to learn and the capacity to reform the governance of human communities living in a given locality. (See figure 16.3.)

Using this analytical framework, we can figure out the types of indicators needed to determine the resilience of a given territory and show how already existing metrics can represent those indicators (table 16.4).

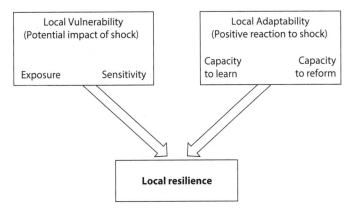

FIGURE 16.3. The local resilience framework. *Source*: Author.

The World Bank has empirically estimated what can separate the study of natural disasters' impact from a conventional income perspective and from a resilience perspective. If the analysis includes "how poverty and lack of capacity to cope with disasters magnify losses in well-being, the effects of floods, wind storms, earthquakes, and tsunamis on well-being are equivalent to a $520 billion drop in consumption—60 percent more than the widely reported asset losses."[25]

We can finally try to assess what the notion of local sustainability might mean. Local sustainability can be defined as maintaining or expanding local well-being under the constraint of its local and global impact (such as waste generation) and local and global environmental conditions (such as climate change). Hence, local sustainability is determined by the global impact of local development (e.g., the way the footprints of London and New York far exceed their municipal boundaries) and the local impact of local phenomena (e.g., climate-change adaptation in Paris). To make localities more sustainable, therefore, means mitigating not only the local impact of global ecological crises and local environmental problems, but also the extraterritorial impact of local development (figure 16.4).

What could be the shape of a local policy driven by well-being and resilience indicators? The Nord-Pas-de-Calais region in France has in recent years combined rigorous research work with real political leadership by involving local residents in innovative participatory practices

TABLE 16.4. Possible indicators of local resilience

	Type of indicator	Example of indicator
Vulnerability		
Exposure	Population concentration	Trade and financial
	Economic wealth concentration	openness
	Geographical exposure (climate, location, etc.)	
	Economic exposure (openness, etc.)	
	Diversification of production systems	
	Quality of urbanism/ construction	
Sensitivity	Human development	Education and health
	Social inequality	indicators
	Quality of territorial preparedness (existence of emergency plans, evacuation routes, conformity with national regulations, etc.)	Gini index
		Local public deficit and debt
	Quality of infrastructures (telecommunication, energy networks, transport, etc.)	
	Quality of first response services	
	Quality of insurance systems	
	Balance of territorial public finances	
Adaptability		
Capacity to learn	Human capital research	Qualification of the labor force
	Quality of information systems	R & D spending
Capacity to reform	Innovation	Patterns data
	Social capital	Institutional trust
	Quality of governance	Quality of government institute indicators
		Territorial fragmentation metric of the OECD Metropolitan database

Source: Author.

Local impact of global crises

Local well-being

Local impact   Extraterritorial impact

Local sustainability

FIGURE 16.4. Local sustainability.

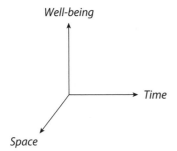

Well-being

Time

Space

FIGURE 16.5. Human welfare in three dimensions.

such as citizens' conferences and hybrid forums to carry several regional projects, including the "ecological and social transformation of the region." It is now recognized as one of the most advanced regions in Europe in the well-being and sustainability transition. The city of Recife, Brazil, has, for its part, created an observatory of municipal well-being, which is also a permanent place of deliberation on urban well-being and its different dimensions.[26] This is at once an exercise in political deliberation, a measurement of well-being, and interpellation of political power. These two examples show what the indicators of well-being and sustainability can bring to the development of localities and how, in turn, localities can contribute to the well-being and sustainability transition.

We have thus arrived, before concluding this book, at an interesting paradox. If sustainability is best measured globally, resilience and well-being are best assessed locally. Human welfare should thus be understood in three dimensions (figure 16.5).

This representation can be understood in two ways. One can break down well-being into current well-being, future well-being (resilience and sustainability), and impact on well-being elsewhere. This breakdown is close to the recommendation of the Conference of European Statisticians, which argues for a distinction between human well-being "here and now," capital (human well-being "later"), and transboundary impacts (human well-being "elsewhere").[27] Alternatively, well-being can be broken down into current well-being, future well-being, and well-being at the local level. In any case, intriguing trade-offs and synergies appear between these different spheres of well-being, which will determine for decades to come the challenges and opportunities of research and policy.

Conclusion

Beyond (the End of) Growth:
Grasping Our Social-Ecological World

While this book strongly advocates disposing of GDP and growth as our guides, they might both be dying of natural causes anyway. The prospect of sustained low economic growth is indeed now part of the landscape of conventional economic thinking, at least three recent interventions bearing witness to this emerging consensus:

Robert Gordon, an early skeptic of the "new economy" of the second half of the 1990s, put forward in the wake of the "great recession" of 2008–2009 the idea that structural forces were countering a real recovery in the United States. According to him, no fewer than six "headwinds"[1] restrained potential US growth in a context of diminishing returns to technological innovation.[2] This analysis almost immediately had a powerful impact in economic and business circles. Gordon's core prediction was that US growth could virtually disappear, shrinking from 1.8 percent to 0.2 percent annually, eroded by rising inequality (-0.5 point), the weight of debt (-0.3 points) and demographic exhaustion, lower educational level, and the impacts of globalization and rising energy prices (-0.2 point each). It should be noted that, in this set of assumptions, the dynamic of innovation is not central: Gordon believes that the slowdown in productivity gain tied to the great innovations of the first half of the twentieth century has already taken place and that it will not rally due to current and future innovations.

Larry Summers, the Harvard economist and former Obama administration chief economic adviser, has revived Alvin Hansen's concept of "secular stagnation" to offer his own account of the end of growth.[3] In his version, structural stagnation has the same implication (a prolonged period of very slow growth), but is driven by very different factors than the ones highlighted by Hansen in the 1930s.[4] First, the growing disparity between earners at the top and bottom of the income distribution plays a detrimental role in global demand. The very rich consume proportionally less of their income than do middle-class or poor people. This drives savings up and global demand down. Second, a buildup in foreign reserves by countries relying on export-led growth rather than domestic demand (such as China and Germany) leads to reduced consumer consumption. This, in turn, boosts savings and hurts global demand. The resulting savings glut exerts downward pressure on interest rates, which makes the returns on future capital weak and limits future increases in demand and investment. According to Summers, fiscal policy—via public investment—is a preferred way for public authorities to breathe life into their sluggish economies.

Finally, in 2014 the Center for Economic and Policy Research published a volume that illustrated the growing number of recognized economists willing to take these analyses seriously and discuss them, including such influential figures as Paul Krugman and Olivier Blanchard.[5] But this is not the first time that the exhaustion of economic growth has been considered a serious possibility by prominent members of the economics profession. In the late 1980s and early 1990s, the fear of a slowdown in economic growth haunted people before it was dissipated by the new economy, which revived the hope that continuous waves of innovation would sustain a regime of robust growth. Likewise, a number of scholars today (such as economist Tyler Cowen) believe that even if a technological plateau has been reached, many innovations are already reviving productivity in the United States and the global economy and will do so even more in the future. These saviors include new-generation automation, biotech and biomedical innovations, and artificial intelligence. After all, according to Robert Gordon's own estimates, the long-term decline in US labor productivity has not been uniform: during the 1996–2004 period (2.46 percent per year), it was actually higher than its 1891–1972 average level (2.33 percent per year), so that it could be revived again.

While interesting, this debate on the demise of growth largely misses the point. The question is not if economic growth is really exhausted and whether we should explore ways to bring about its supposedly desirable return, but to recognize that, even if this happens, it will not result in prosperity for people or sustainability for societies. In other words, regardless of the actual level of growth in the coming years, growth is indeed exhausted as a collective horizon.

Two lines of analysis thus emerge. The first recognizes the depletion of the substance of economic growth but refuses to acknowledge the end of its social relevance and therefore proposes to try to boost it by all means necessary, including by lowering well-being and derailing sustainability. The pro-growth policy agenda in the United States is now centered on "cut and extract" strategies whereby taxes on businesses and high-income individuals are lowered while natural resources overexploitation is encouraged. The second position recognizes both the exhaustion of substance and meaning of economic growth and therefore proposes to replace it as a social project by three alternative objectives: individual and collective well-being, resilience, and sustainability.

This book clearly embraces the latter position and has offered analytical frameworks, instruments, and institutional means to move forward with the transition. It has tried to show that economics should refocus its attention and energy on achieving well-being and sustainability, not growth. This transition is actually already under way, and none other than the two most important economic powers of our world are proof of that dynamic. In the United States, the concern about inequality is gradually supplanting the drive for growth, while China is exiting hypergrowth to try to become more sustainable.

It is now abundantly clear that in the United States, the focus on growth has veiled the inequality crisis. While John F. Kennedy talked about a rising tide that lifts all boats, Barack Obama warned of the "dangerous and growing inequality and lack of upward mobility that has jeopardized middle-class America's basic bargain—that if you work hard, you have a chance to get ahead" and talked about the inequality crisis as "the defining challenge of our time."[6] The fact that a new administration, which owes its accession to power to the severity of the inequality crisis in the United States, is temporarily taking the country backwards on this topic, as on so many others, won't erase the progress in knowledge that has been accomplished.

In China, what looks like an economic crisis is really a transition away from industry and export-led growth and also from hypergrowth.

In the words of former Premier Wen Jiabao (2007): "China's economic growth is unsteady, unbalanced, uncoordinated, and unsustainable." Going further, Li Keqiang, China's prime minister, acknowledged in a press conference on March 13, 2014 in Beijing, "What we care more about is the livelihood of our people behind a GDP figure and employment behind GDP growth," adding, to the surprise of many, "We are not preoccupied with GDP growth. The GDP growth we want is one that brings real benefits to our people, helps raise the quality and efficiency of economic development, and contributes to energy conservation and environmental protection." The nation's thirteenth five-year plan, released in November of 2015, includes targets of "moderately prosperous society" by 2020 and talks about "slower yet healthier economic growth." It also mentions that the need to create a new "ecological civilization" rather than focusing on the GDP growth will become a new priority of the Chinese government. In other words, while GDP continues to be the perilous obsession of Europe, the United States and China are quietly embracing the well-being and sustainability transition by recognizing that GDP is not a trustworthy compass for policy.

But once GDP has been empirically invalidated, a fundamental challenge remains: how to get rid of the mythology of growth. Going beyond growth as a social project does not only mean complementing and eventually replacing GDP with indicators of well-being, resilience, and sustainability. It also implies linking those three objectives in a new shared, positive narrative and building robust institutions to sustain it. Ideas are rendered obsolete not by facts, but by other ideas. How can we embed the indicators of well-being and sustainability that have been put forth in this book in a new narrative as powerful as growth so that they change our view of the economic world for good? What kind of institutions can we imagine to give life to this new vision?

Clarity is needed as to the nature of the well-being and sustainability transition. As a first step toward this end, two mistaken representations of transition should be dispelled. The first way of thinking about transition features a purely cerebral world in which scientists, increasingly convinced that they are on the path to truth, seek to inform ignorant citizens about the gravity of contemporary ecological crises. Science alerts us to the facts, but while this is a significant step forward, it is not enough to change hearts and minds and to eventually alter the course of policy. Warning of the need to change behaviors can actually be counterproductive if this is perceived by ordinary citizens as intellectual arrogance on the part of elites. Transition will not be achieved via obedience. The second features a social world animated by fear of disaster, the claim here being that human societies, subject to a reptilian reflex, will accept change not as a result of conscious understanding, but through a process of disaster-induced learning. Fear is supposed to be a powerful driver of action. In reality it probably engenders paralysis: the more we are told that the end of the world is nigh, that catastrophe beckons, the more we are encouraged to behave irresponsibly. Transition will not be achieved through terror.

What we are left with are three certainties. First of all, the well-being and sustainability transition is possible, as evidenced by innumerable positive transitions of the past that were the fruit of protracted, uneven, and imperfect processes: the abolition of slavery, for instance, or the recognition of women's rights. (Consider also the major structural transitions of human societies observed across the globe in the form of demographic transitions or transitions to freedom.) Second, this transition will entail a voluntary change in behaviors and attitudes beyond pure reason or blind panic. (No transition achieved through force will prove lasting.) Third, this transition will be gradual; it will need to take shape over time, growing out of painstakingly constructed and mutually reinforcing institutions. There can be no magic leap from one state of society to another.

If it is to become a social reality, the well-being and sustainability transition will thus result from a combination of both knowledge and belief. If the necessity of its adoption is generated by knowledge, its possibility will emerge from the social belief that alone instills the power to set common action in motion. It is necessary first to know, and then to believe—even, in some cases, to dream—in order eventually to act.

The common positive narrative of this transition cannot be constructed exclusively upon the imperative of economic efficiency. The transition must be fair but also stable and protective. If "growth" cannot help us solve the two major crises of the early twenty-first century, the inequality crisis and ecological crises, bringing together our understanding of them can put us on the path to resolving both. This is the meaning of a social-ecological view of our world: it makes environmental sense to mitigate our social crisis and social sense to mitigate our environmental crises. In the words of Pope Francis, who decided to put the encyclical *Laudato si*, published in June 2015, under the auspices of St. Francis of Assisi (friend of the poor and author of the Canticle of Brother Sun and Sister Moon, declared patron of ecologists by Pope John Paul II in 1979): "We are faced not with two separate crises, one environmental and the other social, but rather with one complex crisis which is both social and environmental."

We can further elaborate on this key point. The first arrow of causality, which runs from inequality to environmental degradation, can be labelled "integrative social-ecology," as it shows that the gap between the rich and the poor and the interaction of the two groups leads to the worsening of environmental degradations and ecological crises that affect every member of a given community (the scale of which can vary from local to global). The reciprocal arrow of causality that goes from ecological crises to social injustice can be labelled "differential social-ecology," as it shows that the social impact of ecological crises is not the same for different individuals and groups, given their socio-economic status.[7]

My final point is thus that new indicators of well-being and sustainability, if they are to change our world, should be embedded in social-ecological institutions. Institutions are the dynamic driving forces of all human transition because their very purpose is to facilitate social cooperation over time. What we are in the habit of referring to as "industrial revolutions" were also—and perhaps principally—"institutional revolutions," from the enshrining of stable property rights in the nineteenth century through the introduction of employment contracts and social protection in the twentieth to the redefinition of property rights in the current era of social networks and sharing economy.

What could be the form of a social-ecological institution? The modern welfare state was devised in the 1880s in unified Germany to forge a new alliance between labor and capital, and was built upon the idea that human beings are entitled to receive protection against the hazards of nature and social life. "Social security"—currently guaranteed to fewer than 30 percent of the world's population in about half of the planet's countries—is already a considerable extension of the "civil security" that Hobbes entrusted to the Leviathan in the mid-1600s. The next stage consists in moving on from social security to social-ecological security by acknowledging that the nature of social risk underwent a fundamental change at the end of the twentieth century. A state fit for the twenty-first century should aim at forging a new alliance between social issues and environmental challenge.

Because social risk today includes a major environmental dimension (floods, heat waves, hurricanes, storms, etc.), citizens are entitled to expect public authorities to develop and put in place adequate means of protection. Because the well-being of individuals and groups is increasingly determined by environmental conditions, it is legitimate for social policy to include the environmental dimension. Environmental crises, in other words, should be considered as social risks and therefore call for insurance.

In fact, whereas "social policy" first appeared as a concept and discipline for study in 1958 in the writings of Richard Titmuss, it was extended as early as in 1962 by Titmuss's coauthor, François Lafitte, to include environmental issues. Lafitte hence conceptualized social-ecological policy by defining social policy as policy relating to the immediate environment. Considered in this way, social policy covers not only the social conditions of life (family, work, leisure) but access to environmental amenities, control of urban pollution, and the whole set of environmental factors likely to influence individuals' health and well-being. There is no fundamental difference between social and environmental policy: both are aimed at correcting the shortcomings of the market economy in situations of imperfect information, incomplete markets, externalities, and the like, which fully justify public intervention.

What might be the role of a social-ecological state? It would be no different from that fulfilled by the welfare state through its functions of allocation, redistribution, and stabilization, but these functions would be applied to environmental issues. Let us consider the function of stabilization. In its traditional meaning, this consists of governments' bringing into play automatic stabilizers (typically income tax and unemployment benefits) and discretionary policy (e.g., the US stimulus package in February 2009) in order to cushion an economic shock and prevent a recession from degenerating into a depression.

The social-ecological stabilization function is, by the same logic, aimed at enabling individuals to deal with ecological shocks by preserving their well-being, just as social protection is aimed at enabling them to preserve their well-being regardless of economic cycles. The stabilization function thus increases resilience.

Embryonic versions of this policy already exist. In the Philippines, a public guarantee has been developed within the social security system to allow residents to cope with natural disasters; according to this arrangement, victims are awarded "disaster loans," or emergency financial assistance at preferential rates. At the global level, efforts are being made in the context of climate negotiations to put in place a so-called loss and damage mechanism to provide assistance to the most vulnerable nations. These mechanisms can be understood as the building blocks of national and global social-ecological stabilization. By the same token, the social cost of ecological crises must be made visible in order to reveal the misguided allocation of resources to which the current economic systems lead, while redistribution should occur among groups that are not all equally vulnerable to global environmental change. A key emerging notion in this respect is that of environmental inequality.[8]

New indicators of well-being and sustainability need the social-ecological narrative to become performative. The social-ecological state could not operate without new indicators of well-being and sustainability. Social-ecological accounting, risk, and insurance could end up reinventing social policy in the face of socially unequal environmental crises just as public policy was reinvented in the last hundred years to mutualize, prevent, and ultimately reduce major social risks all over the world. Then the transition toward well-being, resilience, and sustainability could become more than a necessity: it would be an opportunity.

Notes

INTRODUCTION: VALUES, DATA, AND INDICATORS

1. Daniel S. Hamermesh, "Six Decades of Top Economics Publishing: Who and How?" *Journal of Economic Literature* 51, no. 1 (2013): 162–72.

2. D. Meadows, *Indicators and Information Systems for Sustainable Development—A Report to the Balaton Group* (Hartland, VT: The Sustainability Institute, 1998), http://www.iisd.org/pdf/s_ind_2.pdf.

3. The lifelong scholarship of the late Alain Desrosières has been devoted to showing that policy indicators are both instruments of proof and power.

4. I borrow this distinction from Marc Fleurbaey and Didier Blanchet, *Beyond GDP: Measuring Welfare and Assessing Sustainability* (New York: Oxford University Press, 2013).

5. From the Internet Classics Archive, http://classics.mit.edu/Aristotle/nicomachaen.html.

6. Jeremy Bentham, "A Comment on the Commentaries and a Fragment on Government," in *The Collected Works of Jeremy Bentham*, vol. 2, ed. J. H. Burns and H. L. A. Hart (Oxford, UK: Oxford University Press, 1977), 393.

7. John Stuart Mill, *Principles of Political Economy with Some of Their Applications to Social Philosophy*, Book 4, Chapter 6, "Of the Stationary State" (London: J. W. Parker, 1848).

8. Remarks at the University of Kansas, March 18, 1968, https://www.jfklibrary.org/Research/Research-Aids/Ready-Reference/RFK-Speeches/Remarks-of-Robert-F-Kennedy-at-the-University-of-Kansas-March-18-1968.aspx.

9. W. Nordhaus and J. Tobin, "Is Growth Obsolete?" in *The Measurement of Economic and Social Performance*, ed. Milton Moss (New York: National Bureau of Economic Research, 1973).

10. Simon Kuznets, "How to Judge Quality," *The New Republic*, Oct. 20, 1962: 29.

11. Adam Davidson, "The Economy's Missing Metrics," *The New York Times Magazine*, July 1, 2015.

12. Among recent publications, see Diane Coyle, *GDP: A Brief but Affectionate History* (Princeton, NJ: Princeton University Press, 2014); Dirk Philipsen, *The Little*

Big Number: How GDP Came to Rule the World and What to Do About It (Princeton, NJ: Princeton University Press, 2015); and Philipp Lepenies, *A Political History of GDP* (New York: Columbia University Press, 2016).

13. For instance, Diane Coyle, *The Economics of Enough: How to Run the Economy as if the Future Matters* (Princeton, NJ: Princeton University Press); L. Fioramont, *Gross Domestic Problem: The Politics behind the World's Most Powerful Number* (London: Zed Books, 2013); Marc Fleurbaey, "Beyond GDP: The Quest for a Measure of Social Welfare," *Journal of Economic Literature* 47, no. 4 (2009), 1029–75; and Joseph E. Stiglitz and Amartya Sen, eds., *Report by the Commission on the Measurement of Economic Performance and Social Progress* (Paris: The Commission, 2009).

14. Obviously, the set of well-being dimensions chosen for this book is not exhaustive and some important ones only alluded to, such as nutrition, housing, or security, deserve more substantial developments.

15. R. Costanza, I. Kubiszewski, E. Giovannini, et al., "Development: Time to Leave GDP Behind," *Nature* 505, no. 7483 (2014), 283–85.

PART 1: THE NEW EMPIRICAL ORDER

1. Adam Smith, *An Inquiry into the Nature and Causes of the Wealth of Nations*, Book IV (London: Methuen; 1904 [1776]).

CHAPTER 1: THE ASCENT OF "DATANOMICS": THE CASE OF THE EUROPEAN UNION

1. Geoffrey Brennan and James M. Buchanan, *The Reason of Rules: Constitutional Political Economy* (New York: Cambridge University Press, 1988).

2. Marco Dani, "Economic Constitutionalism(s) in a Time of Uneasiness: Comparative Study on the Economic Constitutional Identities of Italy, the WTO and the EU," Jean Monnet Working Paper 08/05 (New York: New York University, 2005); Miguel Poiares Maduro, *We the Court: The European Court of Justice and the European Economic Constitution* (Oxford, UK: Hart Publishing, 1998).

3. This conception was formally advanced by Finn Kydland and Edward Prescott (1977) and Brennan and Buchanan (1988), who intended to develop and legitimize, on behalf of individual freedoms and the effectiveness of public policy, an economic constitutional order constraining the state's power. According to this perspective, public policies ought to be governed by principles with which the state cannot interfere. See Finn E. Kydland and Edward C. Prescott, "Rules Rather than Discretion: The Inconsistency of Optimal Plans," *Journal of Political Economy* 85, no. 3 (1977): 473–91; and Brennan and Buchanan, *The Reason of Rules*.

4. The EU's fiscal rules have been amended in recent years, but the philosophy of the Stability Pact remains. Recent reforms include the European Union Fiscal

Treaty (in full, the "Treaty on Stability, Coordination and Governance"), which was signed by only 25 EU member states on March 2, 2012 and ratified by the national parliaments, which set an agenda for fiscal consolidation that might prove too drastic for many member states in the current economic conditions and eventually prevent the reduction of public deficit and debt.

5. Jacques Le Cacheux and Éloi Laurent, *The State of the European Union*, Vol. 4: *From Crisis to Sustainability* (Basingstoke: Palgrave Macmillan, 2014).

6. "The New Sick Man of Europe: the European Union," Pew Research Center Commentary, May 13, 2013, http://www.pewglobal.org/2013/05/13/the -new-sick-man-of-europe-the-european-union/.

7. As we will see in the chapter devoted to work, the unemployment rate is not an indicator without limits, but its dynamic generally reflects well the economic policy response to a macroeconomic shock.

8. Le Cacheux and Laurent, *State of the European Union*.

9. The communication identified five key actions for the short- to medium-term: complement GDP with environmental and social indicators (environmental index and quality of life and well-being); provide near real-time information for decision making; report more accurately on distribution and inequalities; develop a European sustainable development scoreboard (including thresholds for environmental sustainability); and extend national accounts to environmental and social issues.

10. *The Lancet* reported that the health of the Greek population had suffered tremendously during the worst of the austerity policy, and even talked about a "Greek public health tragedy." HIV incidence in injectable-drug users rose more than tenfold from 2009 to 2012 and tuberculosis incidence in this population more than doubled in 2013; state funding for mental health decreased by 55 percent between 2011 and 2012; major depression grew to two and a half times its 2008 rate by 2011; suicides increased by 45 percent between 2007 and 2011; and infant mortality jumped by 43 percent between 2008 and 2010. See Alexander Kentikelenis et al., "Greece's Health Crisis: From Austerity to Denialism," *The Lancet* 383, no. 9918 (2014): 748–53.

11. By the same token, in July 2016 the EU triggered the sanction mechanisms of the Stability Pact against Portugal and Spain for failing to respect deficit reduction targets, while the two countries were still economically and politically very weak.

CHAPTER 2: GOOD AND BAD INDICATORS: THE CASE OF GDP

1. See http://www.nobelprize.org/nobel_prizes/economic-sciences/laureates /1984/stone-lecture.pdf; http://www.policysciences.org/classics/preview .pdf and http://www.istp.ethz.ch/content/dam/ethz/special-interest/gess /cis/international-relations-dam/Teaching/cornerstone/Bardach.pdf.

2. There are many possibilities to apply chosen weights to different data, while normalization allows merging data with different units into a consistent index. Normalization is done according to a standard formula that converts the original values of the indicators into numbers within a range of 0 (for the worst possible outcome) and 1 (for the best possible outcome). The formula is: (value to convert − minimum value) / (maximum value − minimum value). When an indicator measures a negative component of well-being (e.g., unemployment), the formula used is: [(1 − value to convert) − minimum value] / (maximum value − minimum value).

3. Simon Kuznets, ed., *National Income, 1929–1932*, National Bureau of Economic Research Bulletin 49 revised edition (June 7, 1934), accessible at http://www.nber.org/chapters/c2258.pdf.

4. Simon Kuznets, *National Income, 1929–1932*, 73rd US Congress, 2nd session, Senate Document 124.

5. J. E. Meade and Richard Stone, "The Construction of Tables of National Income, Expenditure, Savings and Investment," *The Economic Journal* 51, no. 202–3 (June September, 1941): 216–33.

6. This has been analyzed superbly by Mark Blyth in his book *Austerity–The History of a Dangerous Idea* (New York: Oxford University Press, 2013).

7. Net national income is defined by the OECD as "gross domestic product plus net receipts of wages, salaries, and property income from abroad, minus the depreciation of fixed capital assets (dwellings, buildings, machinery, transport equipment, and physical infrastructure) through wear and tear and obsolescence." It was first described in Martin L. Weitzman, "On the Welfare Significance of National Product in a Dynamic Economy," *The Quarterly Journal of Economics* 90, no. 1 (1976): 156–62.

8. While GDP is an indicator that counts economic activity within a country whether it results from nationals and foreigners and neglects national wealth creation beyond the country's borders, GNP counts only nationals' economic activity within the country's borders and adds the contribution of nationals abroad.

9. Diane Coyle, *GDP: A Brief but Affectionate History* (Princeton, NJ: Princeton University Press, 2014).

10. As reported by Reuters, "China Minister Warns Pollution, Waste Imperil Growth," February 28, 2011, http://www.reuters.com/article/us-china-environment-idUSTRE71R21020110228.

PART II: MAPPING AND MEASURING WELL-BEING
AND SUSTAINABILITY IN THE
TWENTY-FIRST CENTURY

1. John Rawls, *A Theory of Justice* (Cambridge, MA: Belknap Press of Harvard University Press, 1971).

2. Martha Nussbaum, *Frontiers of Justice: Disability, Nationality, Species Member-ship* (Cambridge, MA: Harvard University Press, 2006). See also Amartya K. Sen, *The Idea of Justice* (Cambridge, MA: The Belknap Press of Harvard University Press, 2009).

3. Elinor Ostrom, "Beyond Markets and States: Polycentric Governance of Complex Economic Systems," *American Economic Review* 100, no. 3 (2010): 641–72.

4. Joseph Stiglitz and Amartya Sen, *Report of the Commission on the Measurement of Economic Performance and Social Progress* (Paris: CMEPSP, 2009), http://www.stiglitz-sen-fitoussi.fr/en/index.htm.

5. Partha Dasgupta, *Human Well-Being and the Natural Environment* (Oxford, UK: Oxford University Press, 2001).

CHAPTER 3: INCOME

1. Simon Kuznets, ed., *National Income, 1929–1932*, National Bureau of Economic Research Bulletin 49 revised edition (June 7, 1934), accessible at http://www.nber.org/chapters/c2258.pdf.

2. Joseph Stiglitz, *The Price of Inequality: How Today's Divided Society Endangers Our Future* (New York: W. W. Norton, 2012).

3. Michael Marmot, *Fair Society, Healthy Lives: A Strategic Review of Health Inequalities in England Post-2010* (London: University College London, 2010). Richard Wilkinson and Kate Pickett, *The Spirit Level: Why More Equal Societies Almost Always Do Better* (London: Allen Lane, 2009).

4. Nolan McCarty, Keith T. Poole, and Howard Rosenthal, *Polarized America: The Dance of Ideology and Unequal Riches* (Cambridge, MA: MIT Press, 2008).

5. James K. Boyce, *Economics, the Environment and Our Common Wealth* (Cheltenham, UK: Edward Elgar, 2013); James K. Boyce, *The Political Economy of the Environment* (Cheltenham, UK: Edward Elgar, 2002); Éloi Laurent, "Social-Ecology: Exploring the Missing Link in Sustainable Development," OFCE Working Paper, http://www.ofce.sciences-po.fr/pdf/dtravail/WP2015-07.pdf.

6. Accessible at http://www.measureofamerica.org/.

7. The income measured here is market income, described later in this chapter.

8. Accessible at http://www.nytimes.com/2014/04/23/upshot/about-the-data.html.

9. Accessible at https://www.gpo.gov/fdsys/pkg/ERP-2015/pdf/ERP-2015-chapter1.pdf.

10. Thomas Piketty, Emmanuel Saez, and Gabriel Zucman, "Distributional National Accounts: Methods and Estimates for the United States," NBER Working Paper, December 2016.

11. It represents the area between the Lorenz curve and the hypothetical line of absolute equality, expressed as a percentage of the maximum area under the line.

12. Over the last fifteen years, the price of housing has clearly increased more quickly than household income in all European countries except Germany,

Finland, and Portugal. This increase is noticeable despite the "averaging" effect of national data that hides significant disparities within countries, particularly between large, attractive urban areas where prices have exploded and depopulated rural areas where prices have collapsed. The 2008 financial crisis marked a peak in prices in several countries (Spain, United Kingdom, Ireland, and the Netherlands) where prices have since fallen faster than incomes. Despite this at-times spectacular decrease, the house price-to-income ratio has not, for the most part, returned to long-term trend levels.

13. Dan Ariely and Michael Norton, "Building a Better America—One Wealth Quintile at a Time," *Perspectives on Psychological Science* 6 (2012): 9–12.

14. The OECD, in particular, has recently produced work on this aspect of income inequality.

15. Gabriel Zucman and Emmanuel Saez, "Wealth Inequality in the United States since 1913: Evidence from Capitalized Income Tax Data," *Quarterly Journal of Economics*, forthcoming.

16. *Economic Mobility in the United States, Report of the Pew Charitable Trusts*, 2015, 1.

17. See Carol Graham, *Happiness for All?: Unequal Hopes and Lives in Pursuit of the American Dream* (Princeton, NJ: Princeton University Press, 2017).

18. Henry C. Wallich, "Zero Growth," *Newsweek*, January 24, 1972: 62.

19. The capability approach was developed in the past three decades by, along with Sen, Martha Nussbaum and James Heckman.

20. *World Report on Human Development*, United Nations, 1990.

21. The need to connect income to actual means of subsistence has triggered new research on income of decent existence. Recent efforts in France to calculate "incomes of existence" have centered on the need to assess quantitatively the monetary income needed to live a decent life. The idea consists in establishing the basket of goods and essential services needed for effective participation in social life, and the amounts corresponding to reference budgets for six types of family configurations. For example, for a single person, the monthly budget of reference drawn up by groups of citizens amounts to €1,424 and that for a couple with two children, €3,284.

22. United Nations Development Programme, *Human Development Report 2015: Work for Human Development: Briefing Note for Countries on the 2015 Human Development Report: India*, http://hdr.undp.org/sites/all/themes/hdr_theme/country-notes/IND.pdf.

CHAPTER 4: WORK

1. Persons marginally attached to the labor force are those who are currently neither working nor looking for work, but indicate that they want and are available for a job and have looked for work some time in the previous twelve months. Discouraged workers, a subset of the marginally attached, have given

a job-market-related reason for not currently looking for work. Persons employed part-time for economic reasons are those who want and are available for full-time work but have had to settle for a part-time schedule.

2. Alan B. Krueger, "Where Have All the Workers Gone?" October 2016, accessible at https://www.bostonfed.org/-/media/Documents/economic/conf/great -recovery-2016/Alan-B-Krueger.pdf.

3. International Labour Organization, http://www.ilo.org/global/topics/decent -work/lang--en/index.htm.

4. Grace Connolly, "Misplaced Management Priorities Fuel Sickie Culture," Investors in People, accessible at https://www.investorsinpeople.com/press /misplaced-management-priorities-fuel-sickie-culture.

5. Alexander Szalai, ed., *The Use of Time: Daily Activities of Urban and Suburban Populations in Twelve Countries* (The Hague: Mouton, 1972).

CHAPTER 5: HEALTH

1. Anne Case and Angus Deaton, "Rising Morbidity and Mortality in Midlife among White Non-Hispanic Americans in the 21st Century," *PNAS* 112, no. 49 (2005): 15078–83.

2. HLY are calculated annually by Eurostat for each EU country using the Sullivan (1971) method; this relies on the Global Activity Limitation Indicator, which measures limitation in usual activities and comes from the European Union Statistics on Income and Living Conditions (EU-SILC) survey.

3. World Health Organization, Social Determinants of Health, Key Concepts, http://www.who.int/social_determinants/thecommission/finalreport/key _concepts/en/.

4. For the United Kingdom: Michael Marmot, *Fair Society, Healthy Lives: A Strategic Review of Health Inequalities in England Post-2010* (London: University College London, 2010). For the EU: Michael Marmot, *Review of Social Determinants and the Health Divide in the WHO European Region: Final Report* (Copenhagen: World Health Organization, 2014).

5. See European Environment Agency, *Air Quality in Europe* (Luxembourg: Publications Office, 2015).

6. Robert A. Rohde and Richard A. Muller, "Air Pollution in China: Mapping of Concentrations and Sources," *PLoS ONE* 10, no. 8 (2015).

7. Hippocrates, *On Airs, Waters, and Places*, 400 BCE, MIT Classics, http://classics .mit.edu/Hippocrates/airwatpl.html.

8. The four main NCDs are cardiovascular diseases, cancers, diabetes, and chronic lung diseases.

9. "Global, Regional, and National Age–Sex Specific All-Cause and Cause-Specific Mortality for 240 Causes of Death, 1990–2013: A Systematic Analysis for the Global Burden of Disease Study 2013," *The Lancet* 385, no. 9963 (2015): 117–71.

CHAPTER 6: EDUCATION

1. Accessible at http://ebooks.adelaide.edu.au/r/rabelais/francois/r11g/complete.html.

2. He notes, "Late remediation strategies designed to compensate for early disadvantage such as job training programs, high-school classroom size reductions, convict rehabilitation programs, adult literacy programs, and other active labor market programs are not effective, at least as currently constituted. Remediation in the adolescent years can repair the damage of adverse early environments, but it is costly." James J. Heckman, "Schools, Skills, and Synapses," *Economic Inquiry* 46, no. 3 (2008): 289–324.

3. Around 510,000 students between the ages of fifteen years and three months and sixteen years and two months completed the assessment in 2012, representing about twenty-eight million of their peers in the schools of the sixty-five participating countries and economies. This is a paper-based test, with assessments lasting two hours. In a range of countries and economies, an additional forty minutes were devoted to a computer-based assessment of mathematics, reading, and problem-solving. Students answered a thirty-minute background questionnaire that sought information about themselves, their homes, and their school and learning experiences. *PISA 2012 Results* (Paris: OECD Publishing, 2012).

4. Ibid.

5. Cliometric Society website: http://cliometrics.org/about.htm.

CHAPTER 7: HAPPINESS

1. Aristotle, *Nicomachean Ethics*, translated by W. D. Ross, The Internet Classics Archive, http://classics.mit.edu/Aristotle/nicomachaen.html.

2. Speech before the convention, March 3, 1794.

3. See Richard A. Easterlin, Robson Morgan, Malgorzata Switek, and Fei Wang, "China's Life Satisfaction 1990–2010," *PNAS* 109, no. 25 (2012): 9775–80. The authors explain this situation by arguing, "The burden of worsening life satisfaction in China has fallen chiefly on the lowest socioeconomic groups. An initially highly egalitarian distribution of life satisfaction has been replaced by an increasingly unequal one, with decreasing life satisfaction in persons in the bottom third of the income distribution and increasing life satisfaction in those in the top third" (p. 9775). In other words, inequality analysis is required to make sense of happiness dynamics.

4. Richard Easterlin, "Income and Happiness: Towards a Unified Theory," *The Economic Journal* 111, no. 473 (2001), 465–84.

5. An even subtler resolution of the Easterlin paradox was proposed by Daniel Kahneman and Angus Deaton, who wrote in a 2010 study, "We find that emotional well-being (measured by questions about emotional experiences yesterday) and life evaluation (measured by Cantril's Self-Anchoring Scale) have

different correlates" and "conclude that high income buys life satisfaction but not happiness, and that low income is associated both with low life evaluation and low emotional well-being" (p. 16489). Daniel Kahneman and Angus Deaton, "High Income Improves Evaluation of Life but Not Emotional Well-Being," *PNAS* 107, no. 38 (2010): 16489–93.

6. The happiness equation tests the explicative power on national average life evaluations of six key variables: GDP per capita, social support, healthy life expectancy, freedom to make life choices, generosity, and freedom from corruption. Social support is the national average of the binary responses (either 0 or 1) to the Gallup World Poll question "If you were in trouble, do you have relatives or friends you can count on to help you whenever you need them, or not?"

7. John F. Helliwell, et al., eds., *World Happiness Report* (New York: Earth Institute, Columbia University, 2012).

8. For instance, the mental health indicator uses a version of the General Health Questionnaire (specifically GHQ-12) developed by David Goldberg. It consists of twelve questions that provide a possible indication of depression and anxiety, as well as test confidence and concentration levels; it is calculated and interpreted using the Likert scale with the lowest score at 0 and the highest possible score at 36. Each item has a four-point scale, but there are two types of scales depending on the structure of statements. Some questions range from "not at all" to "much more than usual" and some from "more than usual" to "much less than usual."

9. In 2015, 43.4 percent of Bhutanese were deeply or extensively happy. The other 56.6 percent of those surveyed were not yet happy and 57 percent lacked sufficiency in the nine domains. The 2015 GNH index is thus 0.756, a notch above the 2010 level. Happiness in Bhutan can be said to have increased overall because of a combination of a slight reduction of unhappy people that has compensated for the higher intensity of their unhappiness.

10. Christopher Deeming, "Addressing the Social Determinants of Subjective Well-being: The Latest Challenge for Social Policy," *Journal of Social Policy* 42, no. 3 (2013): 541–65, accessible at http://www.ncbi.nlm.nih.gov/pmc/articles /PMC3663082.

11. Easterlin, "Income and Happiness."

12. "Measuring National Well-Being: Personal Well-Being in the UK, 2014 to 2015," accessible at http://www.ons.gov.uk/peoplepopulationandcommunity /wellbeing/bulletins/measuringnationalwellbeing/2015-09-23.

13. Amartya Sen, *On Ethics and Economics* (Oxford, UK: Basil Blackwell, 1987).

CHAPTER 8: TRUST

1. Paul Seabright, *The Company of Strangers: A Natural History of Economic Life*, second edition (Princeton, NJ: Princeton University Press, 2010).

2. Georg Simmel, *The Philosophy of Money* (London: Routledge, 2011 [1900]), 191.

3. Kenneth J. Arrow, *The Limits of Organization* (New York: W. W. Norton, 1974).

4. Georg Simmel, "The Sociology of Secrecy and of Secret Societies," *American Journal of Sociology* 11 (1906): 441–98.

5. "Community," http://www.oecdbetterlifeindex.org/topics/community/.

6. Social networks are being redefined by the current technological revolution and create new metrics such as "friends" on Facebook and "followers" on Twitter.

7. *R* receives a £10 banknote at the onset of a professional interviewer's visit to his (or her) home; it is described as compensation for taking part in the interview-cum-experiment. *R* is told that he will have the opportunity to obtain £22 if he gives the money to another person (*E*) with whom he has been randomly matched, and about whom he is told nothing. He is told that the experimenter will increase the amount given to *E* to £40 and then will offer *E* the choice either to pay back £22 to *R*, or to keep all £40. Forty-three percent of *R*s passed along £10 ("trusted"), and 50 percent of *E*s returned the specified £22 (were "trustworthy"). John Ermisch, et al., "Measuring People's Trust," *Journal of the Royal Statistical Society: Series A (Statistics in Society)* 172, no. 4 (2009): 749–69.

8. Pascal Perrineau, *Scènes de confiance* (Paris: Textuel, 2012).

CHAPTER 9: INSTITUTIONS

1. Douglass C. North, "Institutions," *The Journal of Economic Perspectives* 5, no. 1 (1991): 97–112, 97.

2. Thomas Hobbes, *Leviathan*, reprinted from the edition of 1651 (Oxford, UK: Clarendon Press, 1909), chapter XIX.

3. "Safety," http://www.oecdbetterlifeindex.org/topics/safety/.

4. On the Freedom House scale, a Free country is one where there is broad scope for open political competition, a climate of respect for civil liberties, significant independent civic life, and independent media. A Partly Free country is one in which there is limited respect for political rights and civil liberties. Partly Free states frequently suffer from an environment of corruption, weak rule of law, ethnic and religious strife, and often a setting in which a single political party enjoys dominance despite the façade of limited pluralism. A Not Free country is one where basic political rights are absent and basic civil liberties are widely and systematically denied.

5. Larry Diamond eloquently writes in this respect, "For a country to be a democracy, it must have more than regular, multiparty elections under a civilian constitutional order. Even significant opposition in presidential elections and opposition party members in the legislature are not enough to move beyond electoral authoritarianism. Elections are only democratic if they are truly free and fair. This requires the freedom to advocate, associate, contest, and campaign. It also requires a fair and neutral electoral administration, a widely

credible system of dispute resolution, balanced access to mass media, and independent vote monitoring." Larry Diamond, "The Democratic Rollback: The Resurgence of the Predatory State," *Foreign Affairs*, March/April 2008: 36–48.

6. Worldwide Governance Indicators (WGI), http://info.worldbank.org /governance/wgi/index.aspx#home.

7. Idem.

8. Ian Morris, *The Measure of Civilization: How Social Development Decides the Fate of Nations* (Princeton, NJ: Princeton University Press, 2013), 6.

CHAPTER 10: MATERIAL FLOWS

1. Václav Smil, *Harvesting the Biosphere: What We Have Taken from Nature* (Cambridge, MA: MIT Press, 2013).

2. Yoichi Kaya, "Impact of Carbon Dioxide Emission Control on GNP Growth: Interpretation of Proposed Scenarios," IPCC Energy and Industry Subgroup, Response Strategies Working Group, 1990.

3. Empirical work on this dimension has begun and first results have been presented in chapter 4 of the UN 2016 Assessment Report for the UNEP International Resource Panel. Results show that, by and large, only relative decoupling occurred between human development and material consumption over the previous four decades. More precisely, the per capita amounts of natural resources required to underpin a high human development level are decreasing over time.

4. Arjen Y. Hoekstra, Ashok K. Chapagain, Maite M. Aldaya, and Mesfin M. Mekonnen, *The Water Footprint Assessment Manual: Setting the Global Standard* (London: Routledge, 2012).

5. Thomas O. Wiedmann, Heinz Schandl, Manfred Lenzen, Daniel Moran, Sangwon Suh, James West, and Keiichiro Kanemoto, "The Material Footprint of Nations," *PNAS* 112, no. 20 (2015): 6271–76.

CHAPTER 11: STATE OF THE BIOSPHERE

1. "During the past two centuries, the global effects of human activities have become clearly noticeable. This is the period when data retrieved from glacial ice cores show the beginning of a growth in the atmospheric concentrations of several 'greenhouse gases,' in particular CO_2 and CH_4. Such a starting date also coincides with James Watt's invention of the steam engine in 1784." Paul J. Crutzen and Eugene F. Stoermer, "The 'Anhropocene,'" IGPB *Global Change Newsletter* 41 (May 2000): 17–18.

2. Will Steffen et al., "The Trajectory of the Anthropocene: The Great Acceleration," *Anthropocene Review*, January 16, 2015.

3. As eloquently put by Vitousek et al., "It is clear that we control much of Earth, and that our activities affect the rest. In a very real sense, the world is in our

hands—and how we handle it will determine its composition and dynamics, and our fate." Peter M. Vitousek, Harold A. Mooney, Jane Lubchenco, and Jerry M. Melillo, "Human Domination of Earth's Ecosystems," *Science* 277, no. 5325 (July 25, 1997): 494–99.

4. The LPI is based on trends in 10,380 populations of 3,038 mammal, bird, reptile, amphibian, and fish species. Trends in different habitats exhibit varying levels of decline, with marine and terrestrial species both showing reductions of 39 percent between 1970 and 2010, while the LPI for freshwater species shows an average decline of 76 percent.

5. Eugene P. Odum, *Fundamentals of Ecology* (Philadelphia: W. B. Saunders, 1953), 9.

6. UK National Ecosystem Assessment (UK NEA), 2011, http://uknea.unep-wcmc .org/EcosystemAssessmentConcepts/EcosystemServices/tabid/103/Default.aspx.

7. Millennium Ecosystem Assessment, *Ecosystems and Human Well-Being: Biodiversity Synthesis* (Washington, DC: World Resources Institute, 2005).

8. Robert Costanza, Ralph d'Arge, Rudolf de Groot, Stephen Farber, et al., "The Value of the World's Ecosystem Services and Natural Capital," *Nature* 387 (1997): 253–60.

9. Robert Costanza, Rudolf de Groot, Paul Sutton, Sander van der Ploeg, et al., "Changes in the Global Value of Ecosystem Services," *Global Environmental Change* 26 (2014): 152–58.

10. The paper's key figures are 45.9, the 1997 figure corrected for inflation; 41.6, the 1997 figure corrected for inflation and decrease in volume; 145, the 1997 figure corrected for inflation and increase in value; and 124.8, the 1997 figure corrected for inflation and then both for increase in value and decrease in volume.

11. UK National Ecosystem Assessment, 2011.

12. http://www.naturalcapitalproject.org/. See also Carl Shapiro, Greg Arthaud, Frank Casey, and Dianna Hogan, "Ecosystem Services Science, Practice, and Policy: Perspectives from ACES, A Community on Ecosystem Services," *Ecological Economics* 115 (July 2015): 1–58; and Stephen Polasky, Erik Nelson, Derric Pennington, and Kris A. Johnson, "The Impact of Land-Use Change on Ecosystem Services, Biodiversity and Returns to Landowners: A Case Study in the State of Minnesota," *Environmental and Resource Economics* 48 (2011): 219–42.

13. Christopher B. Field, Vicente R. Barros, et al., "Summary for Policymakers," in *Climate Change 2014: Impacts, Adaptation, and Vulnerability. Part A: Global and Sectoral Aspects. Contribution of Working Group II to the Fifth Assessment Report of the Intergovernmental Panel on Climate Change* (Cambridge, UK: Cambridge University Press, 2014): 1–32.

14. Marine absorption of carbon is a major problem in its own right, as it increases the acidification of seas and oceans.

15. Michael R. Raupach et al., "Sharing a Quota on Cumulative Carbon Emissions," *Nature Climate Change* 4 (2014): 873–79.

16. Paul Baer, Tom Athanasiou, and Sivan Kartha, *The Greenhouse Development Rights Framework: The Right to Development in a Climate Constrained*

World (Berlin: Heinrich Böll Foundation, Christian Aid, EcoEquity, and the Stockholm Environment Institute, 2014), available online at http://www .GreenhouseDevelopmentRights.org.

17. This criterion is doubly relevant, first from a physical point of view, given the long persistence of certain greenhouse gases in the atmosphere, CO_2 in particular. (The blocking effect of infrared rays in the lower layers of the atmosphere by CO_2 is estimated to be around a hundred years.) Past emissions, therefore, have an effect on current and future climate change. In addition, these past emissions have served the economic development of the nations involved and have increased their adaptation and mitigation capabilities. But at what date should we start accounting for emissions of greenhouse gases? One can imagine many possibilities. The most intuitive is the mid-nineteenth century, when the first significant emissions of greenhouse gases by humans took place. But at that time, knowledge about climate change and its effects was very limited. We cannot, strictly speaking, talk about responsibility in the moral sense before 1990, when the first report of the IPCC (very cautious in its conclusions and recommendations) was published.

18. Will Steffen et al., "Planetary Boundaries," *Science* 347, no. 6223 (Feb. 13, 2015), 1259855-2.

CHAPTER 12: ENVIRONMENTAL PERFORMANCE

1. Initially developed at the University of British Columbia by William Rees and Mathis Wackernagel.

2. For a proposal of carbon pricing, see Stéphane Dion and Éloi Laurent, *Climate Action beyond the Paris Accord*, OFCE Working Paper 2015-22, 2015.

3. See http://sedac.ciesin.columbia.edu/data/collection/esi/.

4. Accessible at http://www.environmentaldemocracyindex.org/.

5. Ida Kubiszewski et al., "Beyond GDP: Measuring and Achieving Global Genuine Progress," *Ecological Economics* 93 (2013): 57–68.

6. Ida Kubiszewski et al., "Estimates of the Genuine Progress Indicator (GPI) for Oregon from 1960–2010 and Recommendations for a Comprehensive Shareholder's Report," *Ecological Economics* 119 (2015): 1–7.

7. *Human Development Report 2010* (New York: United Nations, 2010).

8. Robert Costanza and Bernard C. Patten, "Defining and Predicting Sustainability," *Ecological Economics* 15, no. 3 (1995): 193–96.

CHAPTER 13: SUSTAINABILITY

1. Harold Hotelling, "The Economics of Exhaustible Resources," *The Journal of Political Economy* 39, no. 2 (April 1931): 137–75.

2. Arthur C. Pigou, *The Economics of Welfare*, fourth edition (London: Macmillan, 1932).

3. World Commission on Environment and Development, *Our Common Future* (Report of the Brundtland Commission) (Oxford: Oxford University Press, 1987).

4. Robert Solow, "An Almost Practical Step toward Sustainability," *Resources Policy* 19, no. 3 (1993): 162–72, 168.

5. David W. Pearce, Anil Markandya, and Edward B. Barbier, *Blueprint for a Green Economy* (London: Earthscan, 1989).

6. See the construction of the Index of Economic Well-Being (IEWB), which tried to capture economic well-being with four dimensions: consumption flows, stocks of wealth, equality, and economic security. Lars Osberg and Andrew Sharpe, "An Index of Economic Well-Being for Selected OECD Countries," *Review of Income and Wealth* 48, no. 3 (2002): 291–316.

7. Elinor Ostrom, "Social Capital: A Fad or a Fundamental Concept?" in *Social Capital: A Multifaceted Perspective*, ed. Partha Dasgupta and Ismail Serageldin (Washington, DC: World Bank, 1999), 172–214, accessible at http://documents .worldbank.org/curated/en/663341468174869302/pdf/multi-page.pdf.

8. Robert M. Solow, "Notes on Social Capital and Economic Performance," in Dasgupta and Serageldin, *Social Capital*, 6–10. Solow points out fundamental differences between manufactured and social capital, observing that the latter has a rate of return and can be assessed by aggregating past investment (minus its depreciation), while social capital cannot be measured in this way.

9. Kenneth J. Arrow, "Observations on Social Capital," in Dasgupta and Serageldin, *Social Capital*, 3–5; Kenneth J. Arrow, "The Measurement of the Economic World," in *Fruitful Economics*, ed. Éloi Laurent and Jacques Le Cacheux (London: Palgrave Macmillan, 2015), 15–19.

10. See Joseph E. Stiglitz, "Formal and Informal Institutions," in *Social Capital: A Multifaceted Perspective*, ed. Partha Dasgupta and Ismail Serageldin (Washington, DC: World Bank, 1999): 59–68; and Partha Dasgupta, "Economic Progress and the Idea of Social Capital," idem, 325–424.

11. Kenneth J. Arrow, Partha Dasgupta, Lawrence H. Goulder, Kevin J. Mumford, and Kirsten Oleson, "Sustainability and the Measurement of Wealth," *Environment and Development Economics* 17, no. 3 (2012): 317–53.

12. Thomas Piketty, *Capital in the Twenty-First Century* (Cambridge, MA: Belknap Press of Harvard University Press, 2014).

13. Other breakdowns are obviously possible, such as considering that together, social capital and knowledge capital constitute innovation capital.

14. Partha Dasgupta, 2009, Nature's Role in Sustaining Economic Development, *Philosophical Transactions of the Royal Society B* 365, no. 1537 (Jan. 12, 2010): 5–11.

15. Richard S. J. Tol, "The Stern Review of the Economics of Climate Change: A Comment," Nov. 2, 2006, http://www.fnu.zmaw.de/fileadmin/fnu-files /reports/sternreview.pdf, 4.

16. Martin L. Weitzman, "A Review of *The Stern Review of the Economics of Climate Change*," *Journal of Economic Literature* 45 (2007): 703–24, available at

https://scholar.harvard.edu/files/weitzman/files/review_of_stern_review_jel.45.3.pdf.

17. Joseph Stiglitz and Amartya Sen, *Report of the Commission on the Measurement of Economic Performance and Social Progress* (Paris: CMEPSP, 2009), http://www.stiglitz-sen-fitoussi.fr/en/index.htm., 154.

18. UNU-IHDP and UNEP, *Inclusive Wealth Report 2014: Measuring Progress toward Sustainability* (Cambridge, UK: Cambridge University Press, 2014).

19. Note that this criticism can also apply to the Human Development Index of the United Nations: the three dimensions (income, education, health) are considered on an equal footing in the construction of the index, so that a decrease in one of them may be compensated for by an increase in another. This problem has been addressed somewhat by switching to the use of geometric rather than arithmetic mean in calculating the final index.

20. I thank Anja Malawi Brandon (Stanford University) for her assistance with this box.

21. United Nations, *Transforming Our World: The 2030 Agenda for Sustainable Development,* 2015.

22. J. Sachs, G. Schmidt-Traub, C. Kroll, D. Durand-Delacre, and K. Teksoz, *SDG Index and Dashboards: Global Report* (New York: Bertelsmann and Sustainable Development Solutions Network, 2016).

CHAPTER 14: VALUING WHAT COUNTS

1. Marc Fleurbaey and Didier Blanchet, *Beyond GDP: Measuring Welfare and Assessing Sustainability* (New York: Oxford University Press, 2013).

CHAPTER 15: ENGAGING CITIZENS

1. The law, proposed by Green Member of Parliament Eva Sas and voted in unanimously by the two French chambers, states that "the Government shall annually provide to Parliament on the first Tuesday of October, a report containing the evolution over past years of new wealth indicators such as inequality indicators, quality of life and sustainable development metrics as well as a qualitative or quantitative assessment of the impact of major reforms of previous year and the current year and those planned for the next year."

2. The CBO was created in 1975 and has since then produced very influential and strictly independent analyses of budgetary and economic issues to support the Congressional budget process.

3. CBO, *Budgetary and Economic Effects of Repealing the Affordable Care Act,* June 2015, accessible at https://www.cbo.gov/publication/50252.

4. SPIRAL, or Societal Progress Indicators for the Responsibility of All, is a method of well-being co-construction based on surveys and civic participations of all stakeholders at the local level.

5. Joan Martinez-Alier, *The Environmentalism of the Poor: A Study of Ecological Conflicts and Valuation* (Cheltenham, UK: Edward Elgar, 2003). See also Joan Martinez-Alier and Stephen Naron, "Ecological Distribution Conflicts and Indicators of Sustainability," in *Political Ecology: Global, Historical, and Economic Perspectives*, special issue of the *International Journal of Political Economy* 34, no. 1 (Spring 2004): 13–30.

CHAPTER 16: BUILDING TANGIBLE AND RESILIENT TRANSITIONS

1. See, in particular, Masahisa Fujita, "A Monopolistic Competition Model of Spatial Agglomeration: Differentiated Product Approach," *Regional Science and Urban Economics* 18 (1988): 87–124; and Paul Krugman, "Increasing Returns and Economic Geography," *Journal of Political Economy* 99 (1991): 483–99.

2. Jan K. Brueckner, *Lectures on Urban Economics* (Cambridge, MA: MIT Press, 2011), 1.

3. Paul Krugman, "First Nature, Second Nature, and Metropolitan Location," *Journal of Regional Science* 33, no. 2 (1993): 129.

4. *World Development Report 2009: Reshaping Economic Geography* (Washington, DC: World Bank, 2009).

5. Alternatively, we can consider two extremes within the OECD in terms of household income per capita. The USA has the highest income per capita of all OECD countries, while Chile has the lowest. An international comparison yields a factor of 3.5 between the two countries. But when intranational differences are taken into account, using interregional disparity as a criterion, the comparison becomes richer and more complex: the difference between the richest regions in the United States and Chile is actually greater than international comparison suggests, while the difference between the poorest region in the United States and the richest region of Chile is less than this difference within Chile.

6. Douglass C. North, "Institutions," *The Journal of Economic Perspectives* 5, no. 1 (1991): 97–112.

7. See *How's Life in Your Region?: Measuring Regional and Local Well-Being for Policy Making* (Paris: OECD, 2014) and http://www.oecdregionalwellbeing.org/.

8. See Éloi Laurent, ed., *Mesurer le bien-être et la soutenabilité*, special issue of *Revue de l'OFCE* 145 (2016). Papers available at http://www.ofce.sciences-po.fr/publications/srevue.php?num=145.

9. Accessible at http://cordis.europa.eu/project/rcn/92010_en.html.

10. Accessible at http://www.measureofamerica.org/.

11. Accessible at http://www.arf.asso.fr/wp-content/uploads/2012/04/rapport finalARF.pdf. See also Pierre-Jean Lorens, Grégory Marlier, and Stéphane Humbert, "Vers de nouveaux indicateurs pour le développement humain territorial,"

in Éloi Laurent, ed., *Vers l'égalité des territoires* (Paris: Documentation française, 2013).

12. Rocco L. Bubbico and Lewis Dijkstra, "The European Regional Human Development and Human Poverty Indices," *Regional Focus* 2 (2011), accessible at http://ec.europa.eu/regional_policy/sources/docgener/focus/2011_02_hdev_hpov_indices.pdf.

13. Saamah Abdallah, Aleksi Knuutila, Tim Jackson, and Nic Marks, *The 2010 R-ISEW (Regional Index of Sustainable Economic Well-Being) for All the English Regions*, Centre for Well-Being at the New Economics Foundation, November 2010.

14. Ibid, p. 1.

15. Alan Morton and Lorell Edwards, *Community Wellbeing Indicators, Survey Template for Local Government*, Australian Centre of Excellence for Local Government, University of Technology, Sydney, 2012.

16. *Personal Well-Being across the UK*, Office for National Statistics, 2013, 1, http://www.ons.gov.uk/ons/rel/wellbeing/measuring-national-well-being/personal-well-being-across-the-uk--2012-13/sb---personal-well-being-across-the-uk--2012-13.html.

17. http://www.equality-of-opportunity.org/.

18. Raj Chetty, Nathaniel Hendren, Patrick Kline, and Emmanuel Saez. "Where Is the Land of Opportunity?: The Geography of Intergenerational Mobility in the United States," June 2014, http://www.equality-of-opportunity.org/assets/documents/mobility_geo.pdf. Quote from Executive Summary.

19. C. Perrings, "Resilience in the Dynamics of Economic-Environment Systems," *Environmental and Resource Economics* 11, no. 3–4 (1998): 511–20, 505.

20. W. Neil Adger, "Vulnerability," *Global Environmental Change* 16 (2006) 268–81. See also Carl Folke, "Resilience: The Emergence of a Perspective for Social-Ecological Systems Analyses," *Global Environmental Change* 16 (2006): 253–67, 268.

21. Romain Duval and Lukas Vogel, "Economic Resilience to Shocks: The Role of Structural Policies," *OECD Economic Studies* 44 (2008).

22. See Peter A. Hall and Michèle Lamont, eds., *Social Resilience in the Neoliberal Era* (Cambridge, UK: Cambridge University Press, 2013).

23. UNISDR, https://www.unisdr.org/we/inform/terminology.

24. Global Environmental Outlook, Division of Early Warning and Assessment of the United Nations Environment Programme, http://www.unep.org/geo/geo.

25. Stéphane Hallegatte, Adrien Vogt-Schilb, Mook Bangalore, and Julie Rozenberg, *Unbreakable: Building the Resilience of the Poor in the Face of Natural Disasters* (Washington, DC: World Bank, 2017), 4.

26. Accessible at http://www.observatoriodorecife.org.br/.

27. *Conference of European Statisticians Recommendations on Measuring Sustainable Development* (New York: United Nations, 2013).

CONCLUSION: BEYOND (THE END OF) GROWTH: GRASPING OUR SOCIAL-ECOLOGICAL WORLD

1. Gordon subsequently refined his hypothesis, arguing that only four of the initial six "headwinds" were really critical. See Robert J. Gordon, *The Rise and Fall of American Growth: The U.S. Standard of Living since the Civil War* (Princeton, NJ: Princeton University Press, 2016).

2. Robert J. Gordon, "Is U.S. Economic Growth Over?: Faltering Innovation and the Six Headwinds," NBER Working Paper 18315, August 2012.

3. He first applied this idea to the US economy in a talk at the IMF in November 2013 and then to the global situation in a panel at the American Economic Association meeting in January of 2014.

4. The original idea of secular stagnation goes back to the work of Keynesian economist Alvin Hansen and his 1938 presidential talk at the American Economic Association annual meeting, describing the economic future at the time in grim terms: "This is the essence of secular stagnation—sick recoveries which die in their infancy and depressions which feed on themselves and leave a hard and seemingly immovable core of unemployment." For Hansen, the key drivers of the inevitable "secular stagnation" of the US economy were its declining population, lessening expansion of geographical territory, and slowing of technical progress. In Alvin H. Hansen, "Economic Progress and Declining Population Growth," *The American Economic Review* 29, no. 1 (1939): 1–15.

5. Coen Teulings and Richard E. Baldwin, eds., *Secular Stagnation: Facts, Causes and Cures* (London: CEPR, 2014).

6. Remarks by the President on Economic Mobility, December 4, 2013, Washington, DC, https://obamawhitehouse.archives.gov/the-press-office/2013/12/04/remarks-president-economic-mobility.

7. On the social-ecological framework, see Éloi Laurent, *Social-écologie* (Paris: Flammarion, 2011) and Éloi Laurent and Philippe Pochet, *Towards a Social-Ecological Transition: Solidarity in the Age of Environmental Challenge* (Brussels: ETUI, 2015).

8. An environmental inequality, which may be the simple empirical observation of a difference or disparity, results in an injustice or is unjust if the well-being and capabilities of a particular population are disproportionately affected by its environmental conditions of existence. The environmental conditions of existence consist of, negatively, exposure to pollution and risks, and, positively, access to amenities and natural resources. The particular character of the population in question can be defined according to different criteria: social, demographic, territorial, etc. See Éloi Laurent, "Environmental Inequality in France: A Theoretical, Empirical and Policy Perspective," *Analyse & Kritik* 36 (2014): 251–62.

Index